CYBER SIDE-EFFECTS: HOW SECURE IS THE PERSONAL INFORMATION ENTERED INTO THE FLAWED HEALTHCARE.GOV?

HEARING

BEFORE THE

COMMITTEE ON HOMELAND SECURITY
HOUSE OF REPRESENTATIVES

ONE HUNDRED THIRTEENTH CONGRESS

FIRST SESSION

NOVEMBER 13, 2013

Serial No. 113–41

Printed for the use of the Committee on Homeland Security

Available via the World Wide Web: http://www.gpo.gov/fdsys/

U.S. GOVERNMENT PRINTING OFFICE

87–371 PDF   WASHINGTON : 2014

For sale by the Superintendent of Documents, U.S. Government Printing Office
Internet: bookstore.gpo.gov   Phone: toll free (866) 512–1800; DC area (202) 512–1800
Fax: (202) 512–2250   Mail: Stop SSOP, Washington, DC 20402–0001

COMMITTEE ON HOMELAND SECURITY

MICHAEL T. MCCAUL, Texas, *Chairman*

LAMAR SMITH, Texas
PETER T. KING, New York
MIKE ROGERS, Alabama
PAUL C. BROUN, Georgia
CANDICE S. MILLER, Michigan, *Vice Chair*
PATRICK MEEHAN, Pennsylvania
JEFF DUNCAN, South Carolina
TOM MARINO, Pennsylvania
JASON CHAFFETZ, Utah
STEVEN M. PALAZZO, Mississippi
LOU BARLETTA, Pennsylvania
CHRIS STEWART, Utah
RICHARD HUDSON, North Carolina
STEVE DAINES, Montana
SUSAN W. BROOKS, Indiana
SCOTT PERRY, Pennsylvania
MARK SANFORD, South Carolina

BENNIE G. THOMPSON, Mississippi
LORETTA SANCHEZ, California
SHEILA JACKSON LEE, Texas
YVETTE D. CLARKE, New York
BRIAN HIGGINS, New York
CEDRIC L. RICHMOND, Louisiana
WILLIAM R. KEATING, Massachusetts
RON BARBER, Arizona
DONDALD M. PAYNE, JR., New Jersey
BETO O'ROURKE, Texas
TULSI GABBARD, Hawaii
FILEMON VELA, Texas
STEVEN A. HORSFORD, Nevada
ERIC SWALWELL, California

GREG HILL, *Chief of Staff*
MICHAEL GEFFROY, *Deputy Chief of Staff/Chief Counsel*
MICHAEL S. TWINCHEK, *Chief Clerk*
I. LANIER AVANT, *Minority Staff Director*

(II)

CONTENTS

CYBER SIDE-EFFECTS: HOW SECURE IS THE PERSONAL INFORMATION ENTERED INTO THE FLAWED HEALTHCARE.GOV?

Wednesday, November 13, 2013

U.S. HOUSE OF REPRESENTATIVES,
COMMITTEE ON HOMELAND SECURITY,
Washington, DC.

The committee met, pursuant to call, at 10:11 a.m., in Room 311, Cannon House Office Building, Hon. Michael T. McCaul [Chairman of the committee] presiding.

Present: Representatives McCaul, Miller, Meehan, Duncan, Barletta, Stewart, Hudson, Daines, Brooks, Perry, Sanford, Thompson, Sanchez, Jackson Lee, Clarke, Richmond, Barber, Payne, O'Rourke, and Horsford.

Chairman MCCAUL. The Committee on Homeland Security will come to order. The committee is meeting today to examine the security of *HealthCare.gov* and the protection of private information of the American people. I now recognize myself for an opening statement.

This hearing is part of our on-going oversight of the roll-out of the Patient Protection and Affordable Care Act, also known as Obamacare. Today's hearing follows two subcommittee hearings held by my good friend, Chairman Pat Meehan on the security of the data hub and health care exchanges. I would note that in those two hearings the Centers for Medicare and Medicaid Services, or CMS, repeatedly assured this committee that the systems would be both functional and secure. Those assurances ring hollow in light of the disastrous roll-out of *HealthCare.gov*.

We are concerned that the security of the system is as flawed as its functionality. The Department of Homeland Security has two roles in the implementation of Obamacare. The first is to verify the immigration status of applicants. We look forward to hearing more about how the system works from Ms. Correa of USCIS, who is with us here today. The second role DHS plays in Obamacare is overseeing the security of Federal civilian networks. We will have some slides up to demonstrate that.

[The information follows:]

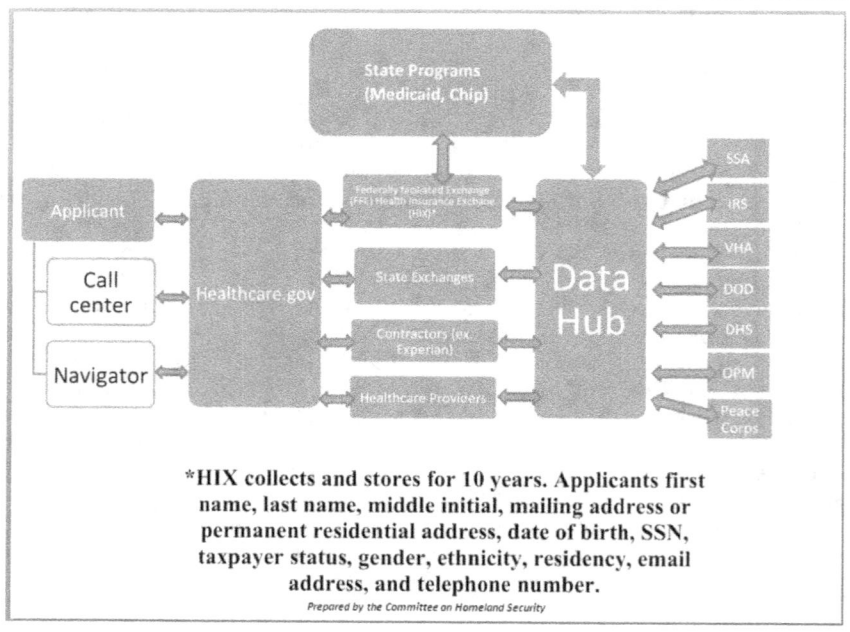

*HIX collects and stores for 10 years. Applicants first name, last name, middle initial, mailing address or permanent residential address, date of birth, SSN, taxpayer status, gender, ethnicity, residency, email address, and telephone number.

Prepared by the Committee on Homeland Security

Chairman McCAUL. According to the Department's website, DHS is responsible for overseeing the protection of the dot.gov domain. That being the case, I think it would surprise many Americans to know that DHS had effectively no input into the security of *HealthCare.gov*, despite it being, arguably, the most significant Federal Government website ever created. To be clear, DHS has not participated in any meaningful way in developing, monitoring, or ensuring the security of *HealthCare.gov*, the health exchanges, or the Federal Data Services Hub. The only contact between DHS and CMS consisted of two e-mails and one phone call.

Departments and agencies are responsible for setting up their own cybersecurity systems. But because of statutory limitations, DHS can only recommend policies and offer assistance on a voluntary basis. In this case, CMS never asked DHS for advice, technical assistance, or even a threat briefing. It is with this limited oversight that the same people at CMS who told us the system would work are telling us now that it is secure. The reason this concerns me is that if customers are able to log on to *HealthCare.gov* they are required to enter vast amounts of personal identifiable information about themselves and their family members.

This information includes their name, addresses, date of birth, Social Security number, citizenship, immigration status, employer information, veteran status, household income, requests for a religious exemption, current health status such as whether or not the applicant is pregnant or has a disability, among other things. While the administration and some of my colleagues across the aisle point out that the Data Services Hub does not store this information, it is important to note that the State exchanges and the Federal exchange servicing 34 States store and keep that information for up to 10 years.

All this information is a tempting target for hackers, identity thieves, and other malicious actors. We already have reported cases of hacks, fraudulent websites, and documented security vulnerabilities in the system. We are also concerned that the so-called "navigators," charged with helping people enroll in Obamacare are not subjected to background checks. This will undoubtedly result in cases of fraud and identity theft, most of which we won't even know about for months.

In fact, just yesterday we received reports of navigators in my home State of Texas encouraging applicants to lie in order to get information—or to get higher insurance subsidies. Even if a system worked properly, the centralization of so much personal data would create security concerns. But in this case, *HealthCare.gov* is so flawed these concerns are even greater. Mr. Luke Chung will testify to shed some light on the technical problems with *HealthCare.gov* and how those affect security, and I look forward to his testimony.

Moving forward, we believe it is vital for the Federal Government to use every asset it has, including DHS, to secure its networks and ensure the security of Americans' most sensitive personal data. As such, DHS needs to have not just the responsibility but, more importantly, the tools and authorities it needs to secure the dot.gov domain. Our committee is currently working on legislation to address this by codifying the DHS cyber mission. We look forward to working with the Ranking Member and other Members of the committee as we move that bill through the legislative process.

With that, the Chairman now recognizes the Ranking Member, the gentleman from Mississippi, Mr. Thompson, for any statement he may have.

Mr. THOMPSON. Thank you very much, Mr. Chairman. Thank you for holding today's hearing. I also want to thank the witnesses for also appearing today.

Understand that this hearing will discuss the Department of Homeland Security's role in the Affordable Care Act. The role played by DHS is two-fold. First, the Department is responsible for verifying that anyone who applies for benefits under the ACA is a citizen or legal resident. This function required by the ACA is very similar to the information required under E-Verify. The Department performs this function thousands of times each day, and transmits the information to any Government agency or employer that needs it.

I am sure we all remember the beginning of the E-Verify program. Just a few years ago, my friends on the other side of the aisle sought to expand E-Verify. At that time, many critics believed E-Verify was a deeply-flawed program that relied on inaccurate Government databases and added unnecessary costs to businesses. We called attention to flaws in the computer systems and databases that E-Verify relied upon. The deficiencies in those systems were fixed.

Today, E-Verify has become an ordinary part of the verification process used by businesses and governments to assure that people are eligible to work in the United States. I do not recall efforts to repeal E-Verify because of its faults. The "save" system used in the ACA functions is much the same way as E-Verify. It seems that my colleagues have expressed concerns about the other role DHS plays in the implementation of ACA. Those concerns have been examined at two subcommittee hearings in this committee.

Based on those hearings, we know that DHS did not have any role in the planning or implementing the *HealthCare.gov* website. Some of my colleagues have indicated that DHS should assure the safety and security of the personal information placed on *HealthCare.gov*. While this is an interesting proposition, there is no law requiring that DHS play such a role. DHS has few responsibilities in the cyber area. First, DHS is responsible for observing, reporting, and acting upon threats to the Federal computer network system.

Second, DHS is responsible for assuring that all fellow agencies are in compliance with FISMA, the Federal law that establishes benchmarks and standards for computer system security within the Federal Government. In sum, DHS is responsible for assuring that HHS followed the correct protocols in establishing the system. DHS would be ready to respond if the system were hacked. But DHS does not have an on-going role with the security of the *HealthCare.gov* system.

If my colleagues believed DHS oversight would be beneficial in assuring the privacy and security of the information contained in the *HealthCare.gov* system, I would suggest that we explore that option. But I am not aware of any law that suggests that the role for DHS, and I do not believe that consideration of such a role is a purpose of today's hearing. It seems that the purpose of today's hearing is to raise concern about the protection of the privacy and security of personal information.

Several committees in the House of Representatives have had hearings on this same topic. Although it is my understanding that DHS has a very small role in assuring the privacy and security of a website established by another agency, I look forward to hearing from the witnesses called here today. Finally, Mr. Chairman, I do not think that the discussion today can ignore the fact that this website was put together using over 50 contractors.

As we know from the committee's recent mark-up of a bill on the Cybersecurity Workforce, the Federal Government is woefully deficient in hiring and retaining cyber professionals. The oversight conducted by this committee over several years has found one IT system after another that has failed to perform or failed to be completed after millions of dollars have been spent. The list of computer failures is as long, and stretches through a few administrations.

The list include SBInet, Emerge, Ramp, and several other IT solutions that did not have names and did not work, but did cost a great deal of money. I am not here to point the finger at DHS. I am certain that DHS is not the only Federal entity that has been plagued by the failure of computer contracts to deliver as promised. So, Mr. Chairman, while I look forward to the discussion today I hope that at some point we can light a candle instead of continuing to curse the darkness.

Those of us in Congress need to come to grips with the notion that computers are not going away, and we must take proactive steps to assure that some office or agency is the repository of cyber expertise and knowledge. That agency must be able to advise other agencies on everything from drafting a solicitation for a computer system to oversight of the installation of the system. It must be the Federal IT help desk and information library. We need to think about new approaches that will save money and work for the American people.

Or we can keep doing what we have been doing: Spending money, making mistakes, wondering what went wrong, and trying to figure out who to blame. Mr. Chairman, the people deserve a Government that stays open, works together, solves problems, and spends money wisely. I think this is the perfect time to show that we are that Government.

With that, I yield back.

[The statement of Ranking Member Thompson follows:]

STATEMENT OF RANKING MEMBER BENNIE G. THOMPSON

NOVEMBER 13, 2013

I understand that this hearing will discuss the Department of Homeland Security's role in the Affordable Care Act. The role played by DHS is two-fold. First, the Department is responsible for verifying that anyone who applies for benefits under the ACA is a citizen or legal resident. This function, required by the ACA, is very similar to the information required under E-Verify. The Department performs this function thousands of times each day and transmits the information to any Government agency or employer that needs it.

I am sure we all remember the beginning of the E-Verify program. Just a few years ago, my friends on the other side of the aisle sought to expand E-Verify. At that time, many critics believed E-Verify was a deeply-flawed program that relied on inaccurate Government databases and added unnecessary costs to businesses. We called attention to flaws in the computer systems and databases that E-Verify relied upon. The deficiencies in those systems were fixed.

Today, E-Verify has become an ordinary part of the verification process used by businesses and governments to assure that people are eligible to work in the United States. I do not recall efforts to repeal E-Verify because of its faults.

The SAVE system, used in the ACA, functions in much the same way as E-Verify. It seems that my colleagues have expressed concerns about the other role DHS plays in the implementation of the ACA. Those concerns have been examined at two subcommittee hearings in this committee. Based on those hearings, we know that DHS did not have any role in the planning or implementing the *HealthCare.gov* website.

Some of my colleagues have indicated that DHS should assure the safety and security of the personal information placed on *HealthCare.gov*. While this is an interesting proposition, there is no law requiring that DHS play such a role. DHS has a few responsibilities in the cyber area. First, DHS is responsible for observing, reporting, and acting upon threats to the Federal computer network system.

Second, DHS is responsible for assuring that all Federal agencies are in compliance with FISMA—the Federal law that establishes benchmarks and standards for computer system security within the Federal Government. In sum, DHS is responsible for assuring that HHS followed the correct protocols in establishing the system and DHS would be ready to respond if the system were hacked.

But DHS does not have an on-going role with the security of the *HealthCare.gov* system.

If my colleagues believe DHS oversight would be beneficial in assuring the privacy and security of the information contained in the *HealthCare.gov* system, I would suggest that we explore that option.

But I am not aware of any law that suggests that role for DHS, and I do not believe the consideration of such a role is the purpose of today's hearing. It seems that the purpose of today's hearing is to raise concerns about the protection of the privacy and security of personal information. Several committees in the House of Representatives have had hearings on this same topic.

Although it is my understanding that DHS has a very small role in assuring the privacy and security of a website established by another agency, I look forward to hearing from the witnesses called here today.

Finally, Mr. Chairman, I do not think that the discussion today can ignore the fact that this website was put together using over 50 contractors. As we know from this committee's recent mark-up of a bill on the cybersecurity workforce, the Federal Government is woefully deficient in hiring and retaining cyber professionals. The oversight conducted by this committee over several years has found one IT system after another that has failed to perform or failed to be completed after millions of dollars have been spent.

The list of computer failures is long and stretches through a few administrations. The list includes—SBI, Emerge, RAMP—and several other IT solutions that did not have names, did not work, but did cost a great deal of money. I am not here to point a finger at DHS. I am certain that DHS is not the only Federal entity that has been plagued by the failure of computer contracts to deliver what was promised.

So Mr. Chairman, while I look forward to the discussion today, I hope that at some point we can light a candle instead of continuing to curse the darkness. Those of us in Congress need to come to grips with the notion that computers are not going away and we must take proactive steps to assure that some office or agency is the repository of cyber expertise and knowledge.

That agency must be able to advise other agencies on everything from drafting a solicitation for a computer system to oversight of the installation of the system. It must be the Federal IT help desk and information library.

We need to think about a new approach that will save money and work for the American people. Or we can keep doing what we have been doing—spending money, making mistakes, wondering what went wrong, and trying to figure out who to blame. Mr. Chairman, the people deserve a Government that stays open, works together, solves problems, and spends money wisely. I think this is the perfect time to show that we are that Government.

Chairman MCCAUL. I thank the Ranking Member. I also want to thank the Ranking Member for his cooperation in holding this important hearing, as well. Other Members of the committee are reminded that opening statements may be submitted for the record.

[The statement of Hon. Jackson Lee follows:]

STATEMENT OF HON. SHEILA JACKSON LEE

NOVEMBER 13, 2013

Chairman McCaul, and Ranking Member Thompson, I thank you for this opportunity to take testimony on cybersecurity as it relates to Federal health insurance exchange.

I welcome today's witnesses:
- Ms. Roberta Stempfley, acting assistant secretary, Office of Cybersecurity and Communications, U.S. Department of Homeland Security;
- Ms. Soraya Correa, associate director, Enterprise Services Directorate, U.S. Citizenship and Immigration Services, U.S. Department of Homeland Security;
- Mr. Luke Chung, president, FMS, Inc. and
- Mr. Waylon Krush, chief executive officer, Lunarline, Inc.

I thank the witnesses for their contribution to committee's understanding regarding the nature of cybersecurity as it relates to personal information.

Today, the House Committee on Homeland Security is holding a hearing to learn about privacy threats regarding the security of personal information provided by visitors to the Federal Health Exchange Marketplace *HealthCare.gov*.

As a senior member of the House Judiciary Committee, privacy protection has been a prominent concern in the protection of women's rights, voting rights, and labor rights.

Today a number of voting rights are under threat because of abusive requirements that undermine privacy rights of voters by requiring that they produce documents proving citizenship, identity, and residency regardless of whether they have an established history of voting or are first-time voters.

Privacy is central to the health and strength of many other rights that we enjoy. Specifically, the First, Fourth, and Fifth Amendments to the Constitution rests on a foundation of privacy protection that allow us to speak as we wish, associate with other, and hold our own beliefs free of fear or threats.

So the topic of today's hearing is of great concern to me. There cannot be privacy without security, although we can have security without privacy. The digital information age requires that Federal agencies must have cybersecurity for any system that collects, retains, or uses personal information.

Privacy protection and cybersecurity are linked in the work I have done on the topic of privacy. The ability to control who, when, why, and how someone else can gain access to personal information requires security. For this reason attention to this issue is central to my strong support for the Federal Health Insurance Market Place found at *HealthCare.gov*.

In May 2006, the Department of Veterans Affairs had a real privacy medical information data breach when a contract worker took home medical information for 26.5 million people.

We are not here today to talk about a data breach of the affordable care website, because they are not storing medical information nor are they storing the information registered on forms. I know this for a fact and not for dramatic effect—I went in search of the facts regarding the website and what problems it was experiencing. I found that there was not a problem with security of the website. There was a problem with capacity and usability of the website and these issues became more complex after launch because the site could not be down more than a few hours each day.

There would be real problems if the Obamacare web registration site collected sensitive personal information on people registering for health care, but it does not collect sensitive personal information.

Sensitive personal information is the type found in taxpayer histories collected over the life time of a person by the IRS. A conversation with a doctor in the examination room is an exchange of highly sensitive personal information. There are no records other than the doctor's notes and that information is not sent to the Federal Government to be stored and maintained for the entire life of a person nor should it be. Most Americans who have take the time to visit the site and look at the information requested know that there is no highly sensitive or sensitive information collected for registering for health insurance.

The real irony of today's hearing is why the registration process for health insurance seeks any personal information. If my friends on the other side of the aisle had not been so over concerned about the verification of income or proof of citizenship then the need to collect a social security number, date of birth, income, place of employment could have been eliminated. The whole process would have worked like every other thing you get a tax exemption for annually. A tax break for mortgage or student loan interest only requires a letter being sent to you for tax records to be sent to tax preparers and in the event of a the rear request for proof of deduction qualification.

I hope that my colleagues on my right will take note that when they insist that a voter must prove citizenship and residency it requires the provision of more personal information which should concern them as much as what is being done at their behest to those seeking health insurance.

When I look at the level of concern you would think that they have held 45 votes to do away with the Affordable Care Act and not one vote to make changes that would address issues that would make it easier to get health insurance. In fact, we are scheduled to have the 46th vote later this week—no help from the Majority just another effort to peck away at the law that they could not end by any other means.

I would offer that if there was no political effort to make something out of the website roll-out there would be an effort to focus negative attention on the toll-free number and if there was nothing negative to say about that aspect of the new law then they would find fault with the application assistance centers.

We are in the midst of a search for a problem that will justify all of the political and financial effort put into stopping a law that the public needs and as people register and share their experience will turn all of this into familiar ground.

The years following the passage of Medicare Part D were rough, because of problems that were fixed with the passage of Obamacare.

There is little if any threat to privacy by cyber threats because of the data practices implemented by the Department of Health and Human Services.

This system is not storing highly sensitive or even sensitive personal information and the personal information it is collecting is not stored. What is being collected is personal information of the type found on a credit application to purchase any product e.g. date of birth, place of work, social security number, income level, and marital status. The information is checked as required by my colleagues on the other side of the aisle and is then discarded.

First, the most important rule for cybersecurity is following the example of the professionals who work in this fast-paced area: Truth comes before beauty. The truth is that there is no computer system that is 100% secure from hostile cyber attacks, natural disasters, structural failures, or human errors.

Second, the internet is a rough neighborhood—the best we can do is to design the best systems possible, provide the resources necessary to follow through on good designs, and ignore the politics of the moment. The most dangerous threats to cybersecurity care very little about anyone's political party. They may care very much about your nation of origin.

Third, cybersecurity is not about the 14-year-old with a laptop, but the botnet attack from a coordinated effort that brings to the discussion significant threats to networks. There is no evidence that nothing occurred that would suggest that the website experienced anything of this nature.

I understand that the interest of many Members in this hearing regarding the health information exchanges may focus on the name of the system, but it is important to note that regardless of the Federal system it is the personal information collected, stored, or used that should be our focus.

Digital records management was of such grave concern to Members of Congress following investigations into the disclosures that then-President Nixon had used his high office to seek out means to cause harm to careers, reputations, and political enemies that the Church Committee conducted extensive hearings on the abuse of power that had occurred.

Due to the revelations of the Church Committee a series of laws were passed by Congress to protect the privacy of Americans and a number of reviews looked specifically at Federal Government use of computers to manage the personal information of citizens.

In 1973, a report "Records, Computers, and the Rights of Citizens" was produced by the former Federal Department of Health Education and Welfare (HEW), which today exists as two agencies—one of which is the Department of Health and Human Services (HHS).

This fact is significant for the topic of today's hearing because Health and Human Services is chiefly responsible for why the United States became the first nation in the world to draft a Federal privacy statute. The agency's role in drafting the

9

world's first Code of Fair Information practice for automated personal data systems places them at the forefront of identifying the important role that computing would play in meeting the needs of a fast-growing Nation, while also recognizing the potential for technology's threat to privacy.

The Code of Fair Information Practices adopted by HEW is based on five principles:

- There must be no personal data record-keeping systems whose very existence is secret.
- There must be a way for a person to find out what information about the person is in a record and how it is used.
- There must be a way for a person to prevent information about the person that was obtained for one purpose from being used or made available for other purposes without the person's consent.
- There must be a way for a person to correct or amend a record of identifiable information about the person.
- Any organization creating, maintaining, using, or disseminating records of identifiable personal data must assure the reliability of the data for their intended use and must take precautions to prevent misuses of the data.

This ground-breaking work informs and guides our hearing today and I want to acknowledge the hard work of the Federal employees at the Department of Health and Human Services who were given little in the way of support or encouragement by the majority of the House in accomplishing a task that was monumental and historic.

Privacy is defined by law. The definition of privacy can be captured under five categories: Physical intrusion, e.g. entering into personal space without permission like someone's home; information intrusion, e.g. accessing documents or information without permission; proprietary intrusion, e.g. using someone's image or name for advertising purposes; associational intrusion, e.g. *NAACP* v. *Alabama* where the Alabama sought the State NAACP membership list; and decisional intrusions, e.g. someone interfering with a woman's personal medical decision making or deciding who can and cannot be married.

The issue of cybersecurity and the Federal and State health insurance exchanges are important and for this reason it is important to provide the American public with accurate and reliable information.

The most important information regarding the Federal health insurance exchange is that it does not violate any of the Code of Fair Information Principles that is central to privacy. There is no secret database; actually there is no database at all. There is a data collection requirement to meet the demands of the House Majority that no person who is not a citizen could gain insurance through the exchange and the second condition that anyone receiving assistance be proven to qualify for that assistance prior to it being provided.

To be honest, if the Majority had not been so insistent on these two conditions the number of questions on the registration form could have been greatly reduced. The form used for registration does not collect sensitive personal information—it collects personal information. Sensitive personal information would be of the type found on individual taxes, which are by law held in secret by the IRS, no matter what someone may say publically about their taxes and the agency—true or not true the agency can never disclose the tax records of taxpayers.

So when we speak of the types and degrees of personal information it is important to know that personal information, sensitive personal information, and highly sensitive personal information are degrees that should be recognized. The health exchanges were only intended and the Federal exchange designed to collect personal information of the nature required by Congress to meet the obligations under the law.

Highly-sensitive personal information would be the type exchanged between a doctor and patient none of which would ever be in this system. This is not to say that cybersecurity is not an issue, any time personal information on citizens is collected by the Federal Government it is an issue that Congress should address by making sure that only what is needed is collected and only retained as long as necessary for a specific purpose.

HHS only collected what was necessary, used it for the purpose of the collection, and promptly discarded that data so no database or system of records was created. This is the most privacy-centric system this committee may have the pleasure of discussing in a cybersecurity-focused hearing. The data practices should be adopted by other agencies that may collect too much, keep more than they need, and use information far outside the scope of the original collection.

The Federal Health Exchange data is only used to do a "handshake" with data in other networks that can authenticate or verify the accuracy of the information provided. This is done in such a way that no data is exchanged with the agency providing the input that the information is accurate. In computing a checksum a mathematical equation is applied to data which produces an answer that will match the same information found in another system. This is just one way of checking information without knowing what the data is and this is the school of thought that informed HHS in developing this system.

The Centers for Medicare and Medicaid Management found within HHS could provide a more detailed reply on the topic of data security in the Federal health information exchange. I ask that the Chairman and Ranking Members both write to the committee of jurisdiction and seek information they may better inform our committee on the details regarding security and the Federal Exchange.

I appreciate the human factors and usability issues with the website, which are being addressed as we meet today. I would suggest that with the new-found interest of the Majority in the customer and user experience that they would focus on redirecting the funding that has been appropriated that would have gone to the States that opted out of the Medicaid expansion be redirected to the Federal.

I am particularly interested in hearing the testimony of the witnesses before the committee who have background and training to speak on the topic of cybersecurity.

Federal cybersecurity is guided by the Federal Information Security Management Act (FISMA). The National Institute of Standards and Technology develop the guidance on FISMA and the Office of Management and Budget provides oversight to assure agencies are meeting the objectives.

Our Nation must continue to improve in the area of cybersecurity and the best approach is build it with the best knowledge we have and provide continuous monitoring.

President Reagan said it best following the Challenger disaster—the shuttle program is one of the Nation's most significant engineering marvels—that after 25 years of space flight, the Nation had grown so used to it that we forgot how recent the Nation had begun to explore space through human missions. He said that the future does not belong to the fainthearted; it belongs to the brave.

He said something that is very important that I will always remember: "We don't keep secrets and cover things up. We do it all up front and in public. That's the way freedom is, and we wouldn't change it for a minute."

This was a very public event, but we will get through it and for the rough start we will learn more than we would have without it and be the better for it.

The first U.S. space station slid out of orbit and broke apart upon reentry into the atmosphere. It failed, but its failure meant that the next time we built a space station is a better space station.

The Swine Flu vaccine miscalculation during the Ford administration, which led to the vaccination of thousands of elderly people for a flu that did not arrive meant that more people died from the vaccine than Swine Flu that year.

The lack of enough Flu vaccine during the George W. Bush administration meant that while nations around the globe had sufficient vaccine for that flu season, we had not ordered enough to meet our Nation's needs.

Like anything in life, there will be rough starts, mistakes, and outright deceptions about the facts. Our strength is in not giving in to the naysayers or negative message peddlers. This may not be in the playbook, but if we lose our edge for taking on the hardest challenges because they are too hard then we have lost something that is truly uniquely American.

I am looking forward to today's discussion and hearing from our witnesses. Thank you.

Chairman MCCAUL. We are pleased to have two panels of distinguished witnesses with us today to discuss this important topic. I will introduce the first panel. Ms. Roberta Stempfley is the acting assistant secretary of the Office of Cybersecurity and Communications at the Department of Homeland Security. In this role, she plays a leading role developing the strategic direction for CS&C and its five divisions. She previously served as the deputy assistant secretary to CS&C and as director of the National Cybersecurity Division. We thank you for being here today.

Next we have Ms. Correa. She is the associate director of the Enterprise Services Directorate at U.S. Citizenship and Immigration Services. She has over 30 years of experience in procurement, Federal assistance, and program management. Before serving in her current role she was deputy associate director for the management directorate, and was responsible for delivering key management and infrastructure structure services to support the USCIS mission. We thank you for being here, as well.

I would like to point out, though, that at this time neither of our witnesses submitted written testimony to the committee before their appearance today, apparently due to their inability to get testimony cleared by the White House. The administration had nearly 2 weeks to provide this testimony, and has been in the habit of providing their testimony after the deadline. Frankly, I expect better, and look forward to receiving testimony on a timely basis as we move forward in this committee.

I ask that the witnesses provide their full written statement as soon as it is available so it will appear in the record. My understanding is that Ms. Stempfley has an oral statement she would like to give, so the Chairman now recognizes her for 5 minutes.

STATEMENT OF ROBERTA "BOBBY" STEMPFLEY, ACTING ASSISTANT SECRETARY, OFFICE OF CYBERSECURITY AND COMMUNICATIONS, U.S. DEPARTMENT OF HOMELAND SECURITY

Ms. STEMPFLEY. Thank you, sir. I truly appreciate the opportunity to provide this opening statement, oral statement. Chairman McCaul, Ranking Member Thompson, and Members of the committee, I appreciate the opportunity to discuss the Department of Homeland Security's efforts to improve cybersecurity posture and capabilities of civilian Federal agencies.

DHS is the lead for securing and defining Federal civilian unclassified information technology systems and networks against cyber intrusions or disruptions and enhancing cybersecurity among critical infrastructure partners. To this end, DHS ensures maximum coordination and partnership with Federal and private stakeholders, while keeping a steady focus on safeguarding the public's privacy, confidentiality, civil rights, and civil liberties.

Within DHS's National Protection and Programs Directorate, the Office of Cybersecurity and Communications focuses on managing risk to the communications and information technology infrastructures and the sectors that depend on them, as well as enabling timely response and recovery to incidents affecting critical infrastructure including Government systems. Additionally, DHS is in the process of setting up critical programs Federal-wide in order to be able to detect and respond to incidents and vulnerabilities, and consolidate traffic, reducing the surface area of possible threat vectors.

With the committee and Congress' support in passing FISMA authorities, DHS and the dot.gov can help to ensure our civilian infrastructure is secured while, at the same time, reducing cost and increasing efficiency with which we are able to work with our agency partners.

CS&C executes its mission by supporting 24/7 information sharing, analysis, and incident response, as well as facilitating interoperable emergency communications, advancing technology solutions for private- and public-sector partners, providing tools and capabilities to ensure the security of Federal civilian Executive branch networks, and engaging in strategic-level coordination for the Department with private-sector organizations on cybersecurity and communications issues.

While DHS leads this National effort under the Federal Information Security Management Act regulations, agency heads are responsible for providing information security protections commensurate with the risk and magnitude of harm resulting from unauthorized access, use, disclosure, disruption, modification, or destruction of information or information systems within their agencies or operated on behalf of their agency by a contracted entity.

Agency heads are provided the flexibility and authority to delegate those responsibilities to the agency chief investment officer in order to ensure compliance with requirements outlined in FISMA and the associated memoranda and directives. These authorities are inclusive of programs to assess, inform, and report on agency status and capabilities relative to FISMA guidance.

While each Federal department and agency retains primary responsibility for securing and defining its own networks and critical information infrastructure, DHS leads efforts in planning and implementing strategic management of information security practices across the Federal enterprise.

The Department provides assistance by collecting and reporting information regarding cyber posture and risks, disseminating cyber alert and warning information to promote protection against cyber threats and the resolution of vulnerabilities, coordinating with partners and customers to attain shared cyber situational awareness, and providing response and recovery support to agencies upon their request. Traditionally, due to current authorities, DHS must be asked by Federal departments and agencies to provide this direct support of independent department and agency responsibilities.

Constantly evolving and sophisticated cyber threats challenge the cybersecurity of the Nation's critical infrastructure and its civilian government system. DHS' responsibility in the breadth of cybersecurity activities and our statutory authorities have not kept up with the rapidly-evolving changes in the cyber environment. While DHS works diligently with our partner agencies and organizations to provide for a secure cyber environment, this often hinders the Department's ability to execute this mission.

The administration has requested legislation to clarify authority, to deploy capabilities such as EINSTEIN across the Federal civilian networks, and to provide operational assistance under OMB's oversight of Federal information technology network security efforts under FISMA, among other things.

We thank this committee for this focus on these important areas. DHS is committed to reducing increasingly sophisticated and damaging risks to Federal departments and agencies and critical infrastructure.

We continue to leverage our partnerships inside and outside Government to enhance security and resilience of our Federal networks while incorporating the privacy and civil liberty safeguards into all aspects of what we do at the Department.

Thank you, sir.

[The prepared statement of Ms. Stempfley follows:]

PREPARED STATEMENT OF ROBERTA "BOBBY" STEMPFLEY

NOVEMBER 13, 2013

INTRODUCTION

Overview of the Mission

Chairman McCaul, Ranking Member Thompson, and Members of the committee, I appreciate the opportunity to discuss the Department of Homeland Security's (DHS's) efforts to improve the cybersecurity posture and capabilities of civilian Federal agencies. Government computer networks and systems contain information on National security, law enforcement, and other sensitive data. It is paramount that the Government protects all information from theft and protects networks and systems from attacks while continually providing essential services to the public.

DHS is the lead for securing and defending Federal civilian unclassified information technology systems and networks against cyber intrusions or disruptions and enhancing cybersecurity among critical infrastructure partners. To this end, DHS ensures maximum coordination and partnership with Federal and private-sector stakeholders while keeping a steady focus on safeguarding the public's privacy, confidentiality, civil rights, and civil liberties. Within DHS's National Protection and Programs Directorate (NPPD), the Office of Cybersecurity and Communications (CS&C) focuses on managing risk to the communications and information technology infrastructures and the sectors that depend upon them, as well as enabling timely response and recovery to incidents affecting critical infrastructure, including Government systems.

CS&C executes its mission by supporting 24×7 information sharing, analysis, and incident response as well as facilitating interoperable emergency communications and advancing technology solutions for private- and public-sector partners. We also provide tools and capabilities to ensure the security of Federal civilian Executive branch networks and engaging in strategic-level coordination for the Department with private-sector organizations on cybersecurity and communications issues.

Roles and Responsibilities

While DHS leads the National effort to secure Federal civilian networks, agency heads are responsible for providing information security protections commensurate with the risk and magnitude of the harm resulting from unauthorized access, use, disclosure, disruption, modification, or destruction of information and information systems within their agency or operated on behalf of their agency by a contracted entity in accordance with Federal Information Security Management Act (FISMA) regulations. Agency heads are provided the flexibility and authority to delegate those responsibilities to the agency's Chief Information Officer (CIO) in order to ensure compliance with the requirements outlined within FISMA and the associated memoranda and directives. These authorities are inclusive of programs to assess, inform, and report on the agencies' status and capabilities relative to FISMA guidance.

Although each Federal department and agency retains primary responsibility for securing and defending its own networks and critical information infrastructure, DHS leads efforts in planning and implementing strategic management of information security practices across the Federal departments and agencies. The Department provides assistance to departments and agencies by collecting and reporting agency information regarding cybersecurity posture and risks, disseminating cyber alert and warning information to promote protection against cyber threats and the resolution of vulnerabilities, coordinating with partners and customers to attain shared cyber situational awareness, and providing response and recovery support to agencies upon their request. Pursuant to current authorities, DHS must be asked by the Federal departments and agencies to provide the aforementioned direct support. The Department focuses its support to Federal networks through the following activities:

- *FISMA.*—The Office of Management and Budget (OMB) has delegated operational responsibilities for Federal civilian cybersecurity to DHS, which established the Department as the lead in promoting and reporting on the cybersecurity posture of Federal civilian Executive branch networks. FISMA requires program officials, and the head of each agency, to mitigate cybersecurity risks based upon its particular requirements. The Department monitors and reports agency status in ensuring the effective implementation of this guidance.
- *Continuous Diagnostics and Mitigation (CDM).*—The CDM program focuses FISMA security metrics on those having a direct impact on Federal civilian departments' and agencies' cybersecurity. By empowering Federal civilian agency

CIOs and Chief Information Security Officers (CISO) with situational awareness into their risk posture and with on-going insight into the effectiveness of security controls, CDM will provide these partners with resources necessary to identify and fix the worst cybersecurity problems first. While this program is in its early stages, we are working in conjunction with Congress to clarify authorities and make CDM fully operational with increased proactive protection of the websites in the .gov domain.

- *National Cybersecurity Protection System.*—Operationally known as EINSTEIN, this program protects Federal civilian Executive branch networks by providing improved situational awareness of cyber threats as well as identification and prevention of malicious cyber activity. While the Department of Health and Human Services (HHS) recently signed a Memorandum of Agreement (MOA) for all EINSTEIN services, HHS is only covered at this point by EINSTEIN 1. EINSTEIN 1, facilitates identification and response to cyber threats and attacks which further enables improvements to network cybersecurity. DHS continues to engage HHS on deployment of other cybersecurity measures based on discussions regarding statutory prohibitions on certain disclosures.

DHS Services

DHS offers additional capabilities and services to assist Federal agencies and stakeholders based upon their cybersecurity status and requirements. The Department engages agency CIOs and CISOs through a variety of mechanisms including information-sharing forums as well as directly through the National Cybersecurity and Communications Integration Center (NCCIC)[1] in response to a specific problem/issue or identified threat. These include:

- *Assessing security posture and recommending improvements.*—Upon agency request, DHS conducts Risk and Vulnerability Assessments to identify potential risks in specific operational networks systems or applications and recommends mitigations.
- *Providing technical assistance.*—DHS may provide direct technical assistance to agencies. For example, by assessing agency compliance and progress in aggregating agencies' network traffic into Trusted Internet Connections, DHS limits access and protects the perimeter of agency networks.
- *Incident response.*—During or following a cybersecurity incident, DHS may provide response capabilities that can aid in mitigation and recovery. Through the NCCIC, DHS further disseminates information on potential or active cybersecurity threats and vulnerabilities analysis to public- and private-sector partners. When requested by an affected agency, DHS provides incident response through the United States Computer Emergency Readiness Team or the Industrial Control Systems-Cyber Emergency Response Team.

DHS Interactions With HHS

DHS works to inform, educate, and increase the cybersecurity capacity of all civilian Federal departments and agencies and has interacted with HHS in the same manner as with all other Federal entities by making available its portfolio of capabilities and services. Although still in the acquisition process, DHS and HHS have entered into a MOA for CDM program while working diligently on the implementation of additional EINSTEIN capabilities. MOA's are a common step taken by DHS as we work to support the cybersecurity needs of our Federal partners, and this MOA is only the latest out of many that have been previously agreed to.

On August 28, 2013 the Deputy Chief Security Officer of HHS's Center for Medicare and Medicaid Services (CMS) initiated a discussion with DHS regarding services that DHS might be able to provide in relation to Affordable Care Act (ACA) systems. Consistent with DHS practice, and similar to actions taken to support a number of other agencies, the Department entered into a general conversation with CMS to refine the request and determine what might be appropriate to meet its needs. Based upon the outcomes of that conversation, further discussions were held and, to date, as DHS does for all Federal partners, DHS has provided descriptions of specific capabilities and services to CMS for its consideration. CS&C has not yet received a specific request from CMS relative to the ACA systems, and has not provided technical assistance to CMS relative to ACA Systems.

---

[1] The NCCIC, a 24×7 cyber situational awareness, incident response, and management center, is a National nexus of cyber and communications integration for the Federal Government, intelligence community, and law enforcement.

CONCLUSION

Constantly evolving and sophisticated cyber threats challenge the cybersecurity of the Nation's critical infrastructure and its civilian government systems. DHS is responsible for a large breadth of cybersecurity activities, yet lacks explicit statutory authority to perform these duties. While DHS works diligently with our partner agencies and organizations to provide for a secure cyber environment, this often hinders the Department's ability to fulfill its mission. The administration has requested legislation to clarify its authority to deploy EINSTEIN across Federal civilian networks and to provide operational assistance to OMB's oversight of Federal information technology network security efforts under FISMA, among other things.

Despite this statutory ambiguity, DHS is committed to reducing risks to Federal departments and agencies and critical infrastructure. We will continue to leverage our partnerships inside and outside of Government to enhance the security and resilience of our Federal networks while incorporating privacy and civil liberties safeguards into all aspects of what we do. Thank you again for the opportunity to provide this information and I look forward to your questions.

Chairman MCCAUL. Thank you for your testimony.

The Chairman now recognizes Ms. Correa for 5 minutes for an opening statement.

STATEMENT OF SORAYA CORREA, ASSOCIATE DIRECTOR, ENTERPRISE SERVICES DIRECTORATE, U.S. CITIZENSHIP AND IMMIGRATION SERVICES, U.S. DEPARTMENT OF HOMELAND SECURITY

Ms. CORREA. Good morning. Chairman McCaul, Ranking Member Thompson, and Members of the committee, I appreciate the opportunity to discuss our shared goals of supporting Government agencies to ensure that only authorized applicants receive public benefits. As the associate director for the Enterprise Services Directorate of the U.S. Citizenship and Immigration Services, I am responsible for overseeing the agency's verification programs. The Patient Protection and Affordable Care Act of 2010, or the ACA, limits eligibility to enroll in a qualified health plan to citizens, nationals, or those otherwise lawfully present in the United States.

The law directs the Department of Health and Human Services to check applicant eligibility against the Department of Homeland Security data if the applicant does not attest that he or she is a U.S. citizen or if the Social Security Administration cannot verify the applicant's claim of U.S. citizenship. The Systematic Alien Verification for Entitlements Program, or SAVE, responds to queries it receives through the hub, a system established by the Centers for Medicare and Medicaid services to help process ACA applications.

SAVE provides the HHS hub with immigration status information and information on naturalized and derived citizens on behalf of DHS. SAVE is a service that helps Federal, State, and local benefit-issuing agencies, institutions, and licensing agencies to determine the immigration status of benefit applicants so that only those applicants entitled to benefits receive them. SAVE does not determine whether applicants are eligible for a specific benefit or license. The benefit-granting agency makes that determination.

SAVE uses an on-line system that checks a benefit applicant's immigration status information against over 100 million Federal records. Agencies that do not have access to an automated system may submit a paper verification request form. SAVE is available in all 50 States. It has been providing immigration status information to public benefit-granting agencies for over 25 years. SAVE has more than 1,060 customer agencies, including the Social Security Administration and most States' departments of motor vehicles.

In fiscal year 2013, the SAVE program received over 14 million queries in our system. Before accessing SAVE, user agencies must sign an agreement with USCIS that details the terms and conditions of their use of SAVE. The SAVE verification process requires up to three steps: Initial verification, additional verify, and third-step verification. For initial verification, a user agency submits a status verification request and the system provides the applicant's immigration status information. If SAVE is not able to verify an individual's immigration status on initial verification, the benefit-granting agency is prompted to submit the query to the additional verification step.

When initiating additional verification, a user agency may also submit additional information to USCIS using the SAVE system. Because this additional verification requires a manual review of available databases the SAVE response time ranges from 3 to 5 Federal working days. If SAVE is not able to verify an individual's immigration status at this stage the agency is prompted to submit the query for third-step verification. To accomplish the third-step verification the user agency must provide USCIS with legible photocopies of both sides of the applicant's immigration documentation.

Registered agencies may submit this information electronically or manually. SAVE response time for the third-step verification is generally 10 to 20 Federal working days. If immigration status still cannot be confirmed, benefit-granting agencies may refer applicants to a local USCIS office to correct or update their records. USCIS and HHS entered into a computer-matching agreement for ACA verifications and tested the web service's connection between SAVE and the HHS hub, including testing of case-specific queries and overall functionality.

After all testing was successfully completed, HHS was granted access to SAVE to meet the October 1 implementation date. SAVE is responding to all properly-submitted queries. As of November 10, 2013 there have been 91,011 hug-generated queries, with an average of 1.31 seconds for initial verification responses. It is important to note that this figure is not a proxy for the number of individuals about whom HHS has submitted queries to SAVE because there are often multiple queries per applicant.

Moreover, this figure is not a proxy for the number of people who have applied for health care coverage under the ACA because only a small percentage of such applicants require the submission of queries to SAVE. To help facilitate immigration status verification for HHS and other agencies under the ACA, USCIS introduced several program enhancements which are not available to all customer agencies. Registered agencies may not receive grant date and sponsorship information for select statuses on initial second- and third-step verification. Previously, agencies has to submit manual forms to request that data.

USCIS also introduced an optional auto second-step feature which allows SAVE to automatically send queries to additional verification if the initial step is unable to verify the applicant's immigration status. This eases burden on the user agencies, and makes the case resolution process more efficient. Additionally, in April 2013 we launched a scan-and-upload feature that enables agencies to electronically attach scanned copies of immigration documents to queries. Since the inception of the SAVE program, USCIS has provided benefit-granting Government agencies a reliable method to verify an applicant's immigration status and to ensure that only authorized applicants receive public benefits.

On behalf of all of my colleagues at USCIS, I am grateful for the opportunity to speak to you today about the SAVE program.

[The prepared statement of Ms. Correa follows:]

PREPARED STATEMENT OF SORAYA CORREA

NOVEMBER 13, 2013

INTRODUCTION

Chairman McCaul, Ranking Member Thompson, and Members of the committee, I appreciate the opportunity to discuss our shared goals of supporting Government agencies to ensure that only authorized applicants receive public benefits. My name is Soraya Correa, associate director for the Enterprise Services Directorate. I am responsible for overseeing verification programs at U.S. Citizenship and Immigration Services (USCIS). The Patient Protection and Affordable Care Act of 2010 (ACA) limits eligibility to enroll in a qualified health plan through the State and Federal exchanges established under the ACA to citizens, nationals, or those otherwise "lawfully present" in the United States. The law directs the Department of Health and Human Services (HHS) to check applicant eligibility against Department of Homeland Security (DHS) data if the applicant does not attest that he or she is a U.S. Citizen, or if the Social Security Administration (SSA) cannot verify the applicant's claim of U.S. Citizenship. The Systematic Alien Verification for Entitlements (SAVE) Program[1] responds to queries and provides HHS, through the "Hub" established by the Centers for Medicare and Medicaid Services, with immigration status information as well as information regarding naturalized and derived citizens on behalf of DHS.

SAVE Access and Verification Process

Before accessing SAVE, user agencies must sign a Memorandum of Agreement (MOA) or a Computer Matching Agreement (CMA) with USCIS that details the terms and conditions of their use of SAVE. The SAVE verification process requires up to three steps: (1) Initial Verification, (2) Additional Verification, and (3) Third-Step Verification. For initial verification, a user agency submits a status verification request and the system provides the applicant's immigration status information. If SAVE is not able to verify an individual's immigration status on initial verification, the benefit granting agency is prompted to submit the query to the additional verification step.

During additional verification, a user agency may also submit additional information, such as a maiden name or additional immigration document numbers, to USCIS using the SAVE system. SAVE response time for additional verification, which includes manual review of available databases, ranges from 3–5 Federal working days. If SAVE is not able to verify an individual's immigration status at this stage, the agency is prompted to submit the query for third-step verification. The user agency must forward a completed Document Verification Request form, with legible photocopies of both sides of the applicant's immigration documentation to USCIS for third-step verification. Registered agencies may submit this information electronically or manually. SAVE response times for third-step verification is

---

[1] SAVE is a service that helps Federal, State, and local benefit-issuing agencies, institutions, and licensing agencies determine the immigration status of benefit applicants so only those applicants entitled to benefits receive them. SAVE does not determine whether applicants are eligible for a specific benefit or license; the benefit-granting agency makes that determination. SAVE uses an on-line system that checks a benefit applicant's immigration status information against over 100 million Federal records. Agencies that do not have access to an automated system may submit a paper verification request. SAVE is available in all 50 States. It has been providing immigration status information to public benefit granting agencies for over 25 years. SAVE has more than 1,060 customer agencies, including the Social Security Administration and most State departments of motor vehicles. The SAVE Program received over 14 million verification requests in fiscal year 2013.

generally 10–20 Federal working days. If immigration status still cannot be confirmed, benefit-granting agencies may refer applicants to a local USCIS office to correct or update their record.

USCIS and HHS entered into a CMA to authorize HHS to use the SAVE program for ACA verification. In preparation for the ACA open enrollment period, USCIS and HHS tested the web services connection between SAVE and the HHS "Hub" that the Exchanges uses to submit queries to SAVE and other partner agencies. The testing included checks on both case-specific queries and overall functionality.

After all testing was successfully completed in the weeks leading up to open enrollment, HHS was granted access to SAVE to meet the October 1 ACA exchanges implementation date. As of November 10, 2013, there have been 91,011 Hub-generated initial queries with an average of 1.31 seconds for initial electronic SAVE responses. It is important to note that this figure is not a proxy for the number of individuals about whom HHS has submitted queries to SAVE because there are often multiple SAVE queries per applicant. Moreover, this figure is not a proxy for the number of people who have applied for health care coverage under the ACA because only a small percentage of such applications require the submission of queries to SAVE. SAVE is responding to all properly-submitted queries.

Program Enhancements

To help facilitate immigration status verification for HHS and other agencies under the ACA, USCIS designated more than 30 additional staff to ACA cases and has introduced several program enhancements. Authorized agencies may now receive grant date and sponsorship information for select statuses on initial, second, and third-step verification. Previously, agencies had to submit multiple forms to determine when an applicant was granted status, and sponsorship information was not available on initial verification.

USCIS also recently introduced an "auto second step" feature, which allows SAVE to automatically send cases to additional verification if the initial step requests additional verification. This enhancement decreases agency user burden, ensures that additional verification cases are referred to the second step, and makes the case resolution process more efficient. Additionally, in April 2013, the SAVE Program launched a scan-and-upload feature that enables agencies to electronically attach scanned copies of immigration documents to cases. Cases with a scanned copy of the immigration document do not require submission of a paper form.

Since the inception of the SAVE Program, USCIS has provided benefit-granting Government agencies a reliable method to verify an applicant's immigration status to ensure that only authorized applicants receive public benefits. On behalf of all of my colleagues at USCIS, I am grateful for the opportunity to speak to you today about the SAVE program.

Chairman McCAUL. Thank you, Ms. Correa. The Chairman now recognizes himself for 5 minutes for questions.

Let me just say at the outset, there have been many Members of Congress on both sides of the aisle who have called for a delay in the implementation of Obamacare for many reasons. But I would think, first and foremost, we have a website that doesn't work. It seems to me it ought to be delayed until that website is functional. But more importantly to me and, I think, many Americans, it should be delayed until we can receive assurances from this administration that these websites are secure because of the personal data that is being put into them, into the exchanges.

We are talking about Social Security numbers, names, addresses, e-mail addresses. You know, we are talking about health information, which is perhaps the most private of all information; certainly information that no American wants a hacker to get access to, to exploit for other purposes. I am personally concerned about the security of this website, and I haven't had the assurances that it is secure. Imagine a hacker getting this personal identifying information and exploiting it for personal gain.

We see identity theft happen all the time, and yet we have this information being plugged into this exchange that I believe is not secure. I believe the American people deserve better. So my first question is to Ms. Stempfley. How many cyber attacks have there been on the *HealthCare.gov* system?

Ms. STEMPFLEY. So thank you for the question. As I commented in my opening statement, the awareness DHS has of cyber attacks that are on-going comes from a multitude of sources. One is Department and agency reports specifically of things that they have identified. We have had a handful of reports from the Department of Health & Human Services—a number of about 16, as my memory recalls. But I will get a specific number for you. As well as identification of threat information either provided to us from intelligence sources or from other mechanisms.

We are aware of one open-source action attempting to perpetrate a denial-of-service attack against a *HealthCare.gov* site that has been successful.

Chairman MCCAUL. So there has been a denial-of-service attack on health care.

Ms. STEMPFLEY. There was the attempt of one.

Chairman MCCAUL. Attempt.

Ms. STEMPFLEY. But it has not been successful.

Chairman MCCAUL. Of course, a denial-of-service attack has the capability to shut down websites.

Ms. STEMPFLEY. The goal of a denial-of-service attack, sir, would, yes, be to deny the access to that information.

Chairman MCCAUL. You know, on the Homeland Security web page it talks about one of your primary missions. That is to oversee the security of the dot.gov domain. Did anyone at HHS—did Secretary Sibelius or anyone at HHS—ever—and involved in this website, and in this roll-out—ever contact DHS about the security of *HealthCare.gov*?

Ms. STEMPFLEY. Again, as I mentioned, the roles and responsibilities between DHS and departments and agencies are split. Departments and agency leadership has principle responsibility for building, operating, and securing their capabilities. The HHS CIO is a member of the CIO Council. Their SISO is a member of the SISO exchanges. We regularly communicate about threat in those forums. We were approached—we regularly communicate about threat and engagement and capabilities in those forums, and we have had limited exchange, specifically with HHS on this.

Chairman MCCAUL. Well, the extent of the conversations that I have seen between HHS and the Department of Homeland Security are two e-mails and one phone call regarding the security of this website. Is that correct?

Ms. STEMPFLEY. It is not typical for a Department or agency, as they are building a specific application, to involve DHS as they build any specific application. So that is an unusual activity at that level. We regularly engage at the Department level.

Chairman MCCAUL. So is the Department essentially defaulting to HHS and Secretary Sibelius for the security of the *HealthCare.gov* website?

Ms. STEMPFLEY. As indicated, sir, under FISMA and current guidance, Department and agency leadership are responsible for securing specific applications under the broad guidance provided by DHS.

Chairman MCCAUL. I believe the oversight of this committee—that you should play a greater role. As your mission statement, you know, accurately says, correctly states that you have the primary responsibility. Do you know what the compliance rate is of HHS with respect to Government cybersecurity standards?

Ms. STEMPFLEY. We have engaged with HHS around compliance against the trusted internet connection activity, and we are in the process of collecting the figures for fiscal year 2013 for FISMA. The FISMA report is traditionally provided to the Hill in February.

Chairman MCCAUL. Well, perhaps I can educate you. It is 50 percent. It is a 50 percent compliance rate. Their score card is 50 percent, and we are defaulting our cybersecurity—the security of Americans' most personal, private data to the Secretary of HHS. I find that unacceptable. Do you realize that 50 percent is the second-lowest score in the Federal Government when it comes to a report card on cybersecurity in the Federal Government?

Ms. STEMPFLEY. I believe, sir, that the scores you are speaking of are the FISMA report from fiscal year 2012 that came forward. Yes, you are accurately representing the scores of HHS in that situation. One of the things you will also see is that HHS has one of the top scores in the implementation of PIV cards, the two-factor authentication. So what is normal for a department is that they will have a range of reporting in that situation. In some instances they will be above average, and in other instances they will be——

Chairman MCCAUL. But do you find it acceptable that you are defaulting to HHS for cybersecurity, when they have a 50 percent compliance record that is the second-lowest in the Federal Government?

Ms. STEMPFLEY. Sir, as your opening statement indicated, we are operating under the current set of authorities and——

Chairman MCCAUL. Well, I hope the Ranking Member will work with me to change that. Because I think you are the department with this expertise, not HHS. I believe you are the one with the—again, the background to fix this. I will just close with this. There was a letter from the CMS administrator to the Ranking Member that basically assured him that they would be following industry best practices and that this website would be secure. I believe that that did not happen.

With that, the Chairman now recognizes the Ranking Member.

Mr. THOMPSON. Thank you very much, Mr. Chairman.

Ms. Correa, in verifying whether or not people who want to participate in the Affordable Care Act are legal or illegal, has that posed a problem for your agency?

Ms. CORREA. Thank you for the question. No, we have not encountered any issues. As I indicated in my opening statement, we establish the connection between the hub and our SAVE system. We tested that functionality and it is working as expected.

Mr. THOMPSON. So those 91,000 queries to ACA have been met without any problem.

Ms. CORREA. They have processed in the manner that they are supposed to process through the SAVE system.

Mr. THOMPSON. Thank——

Ms. CORREA. So in other words, they will come through for initial verification. If we, for some reason, cannot confirm that immigration status, then we prompt them to refer to second step, and so on. So it is functioning as expected.

Mr. THOMPSON. Thank you.

Ms. Stempfley, with respect to the potential for hacking or whatever, do you have any knowledge about the number of attempts that are made daily on the Federal system?

Ms. STEMPFLEY. Sir, just to give you an order of magnitude, in fiscal year 2013 we processed more than 13,800—138,000, excuse me, 138,000 reports to U.S. sort-of attempts against both Federal Government and critical infrastructure systems. So the multitude is fairly substantial.

Mr. THOMPSON. So 138,000 attempts is a big number.

Ms. STEMPFLEY. It is, sir.

Mr. THOMPSON. To your knowledge, have we met the defense requirement to not allow those attempts to be successful? Do we have any kind of——

Ms. STEMPFLEY. I am happy to provide for you, sir, as a response for the record the number of successful compromises that may have occurred. I don't have that number in my brain at the moment.

Mr. THOMPSON. Please provide that to the committee, if you would. With respect to the dot.gov domain and its responsibilities that you have, are you presently carrying that dot.gov domain oversight out?

Ms. STEMPFLEY. Yes, sir.

Mr. THOMPSON. Now, with respect to the *HealthCare.gov* domain, can you, for the committee, share the difference in oversight on that?

Ms. STEMPFLEY. If I understand your question, sir, we provide for example, for FISMA, we provide details to departments and agencies about how to report their compliance with FISMA both in terms of how to specifically answer the FISMA questions and measures, and how frequently to provide those updates so that we can produce the annual report and assessment that is delivered to the Hill in February.

Mr. THOMPSON. Explain to the committee the FISMA requirement; what FISMA is and what is required.

Ms. STEMPFLEY. Certainly. So FISMA lays out a broad set of requirements for departments and agencies to secure their applications and systems. It empowers Department leadership to make local risk decisions about when something may—when a decision about what may need to be—what may be appropriate for a system or application needs to be looked at. You take into account the risk environment that the system operates in. Is it operating inside the department, or is it a heavily-connected system.

Is it containing, for example, intellectual property information or something of that sort. So you are empowered—the departments and agencies are empowered to make those local risk decisions. It requires things such as training of all of your workforce against cybersecurity activity, assurance of accreditation decisions made, and number of systems and applications operating under a range of accreditation decisions.

Mr. THOMPSON. To your knowledge, in the *HealthCare.gov* review, have you provided that training to the individuals with the responsibility for looking at that?

Ms. STEMPFLEY. Again, sir, each department and agency is responsible for providing that training, for ensuring that training is received in there. Then that is reported through the annual report to the Department of Homeland Security, the compliance measures associated with that. So it isn't a—it is not typical for the Department of Homeland Security to provide specific training to a department.

Mr. THOMPSON. But they report the training to you.

Ms. STEMPFLEY. They do. They——

Mr. THOMPSON. You put it in a report.

Ms. STEMPFLEY. We do. At the end of the year, we are—as I indicated, we are in the midst of collecting the fiscal year 2013 data, and the FISMA report is traditionally handed to the Hill in February.

Mr. THOMPSON. Thank you.

Ms. STEMPFLEY. You are welcome.

Mr. THOMPSON. I yield back.

Chairman MCCAUL. I thank the Ranking Member.

The Chairman will recognize other Members for 5 minutes for questions, in accordance with out committee rules. I plan to recognize Members who were present at the start of the hearing by seniority on the committee. Those coming in after the hearing will be recognized in order of arrival.

The Chairman now recognizes the Chairman of the Subcommittee on Cybersecurity, Infrastructure Protection, and Security Technologies, who has held two previous hearings on this issue, Mr. Meehan.

Mr. MEEHAN. I thank you, Mr. Chairman. I thank you, Secretary Stempfley, for your continued work in this area. You know, I am just gonna follow on the question with regard to your being consulted, and giving to the agencies the ability for them to outline the security for their systems. Now, I would suggest to you—and would you not agree—that this is perhaps some of the most important information that is being collected by the Government today: The private identifying information on Americans who are applying, oftentimes giving intimate details about their families, and otherwise to the Government?

Ms. STEMPFLEY. So the—certainly, the Federal Government, through a range of departments, has information about——

Mr. MEEHAN. Well, I mean, the PII is significant information, is it not, Ms. Stempfley?

Ms. STEMPFLEY. PII is certainly important, sir.

Mr. MEEHAN. The Department itself lays out the qualifications. So here I hold in my hand what was created by HHS for the health insurance marketplace, the navigators' standard operating procedures manual. To the best of our review, the only security information developed is to make sure that you don't leave copies of things out on copiers. But under this manual, as was stated by the Secretary herself, it is possible that a felon may be a navigator.

Should there have been guidelines to do security checks on the backgrounds of people who will be in privity of communication with the very applicants? Some of those navigators, under the Secretary's own admission, may be felons?

Ms. STEMPFLEY. Sir, respectfully, I believe that question is best addressed to the Department of Health & Human Services. I am in an area outside——

Mr. MEEHAN. I would like to ask but we don't get them in front of us. I am grateful for your—the—I want to follow up on this other issue, as well, with regard to the compliance with FISMA. Now, we have had quite a go-around, as the Chairman has stated, with representatives before us from HHS. The requirement under FISMA to do the appropriate testing, then to then make sure that they correct any problems that they see. Then, ultimately, give an authorization.

As you know, the inspector general themselves, the Department of Inspector General, released a report in late summer suggesting that there was no window. That the only certification, according to their schedule, was going to happen the day before the operation of the website. Then suddenly, voila! In the middle of the summer, HHS purportedly made these huge leaps, in which they were able to suddenly certify the security of the system.

Now, how is it that they would have been able to go from the period in which they were being—the IG was concerned they weren't even going to be able to meet the deadline until the day before, and suddenly there was tremendous security steps taken by an agency that hadn't done anything for 3 years?

Ms. STEMPFLEY. Sir, the Department of Homeland Security is not generally engaged as a specific application is built or operated. You are asking me a question that I couldn't possibly know the answer to.

Mr. MEEHAN. Okay. Well, one of the things, as the HHS inspector general's report itself says, that the security controls and security testing notwithstanding, they may—the authorizing official may grant security authorization with the knowledge that there are still risks that have not been fully addressed at the time of authorization. Is it possible that this was granted with the recognition that there were still risks, significant risks, that had not been addressed at the time of the authorization?

Ms. STEMPFLEY. The terms of FISMA enable Department leadership to delegate the responsibility for risk assessment and risk acceptance to lower levels. So it is certainly feasible that in that delegation that is——

Mr. MEEHAN. So who is making the determination, then, on the most significant information, the biggest collection of privately-identifying information, that will be collected by the Government anywhere in its history? That is not my words; that is the testimony of others. This is being delegated to people we don't even know?

Ms. STEMPFLEY. Sir, I don't—one of the things that FISMA does not require is awareness of who the accrediting officials are to the Department of Homeland Security. So I am not aware of who the accrediting——

Mr. MEEHAN. So who made the decisions, in other words? We don't know who is making the decisions to authorize the ability to suggest that they have complied with FISMA, when the inspector general themselves said it was going to be unlikely that they could before the start?

Ms. STEMPFLEY. Again, respectfully, sir, that question is best addressed to the Department of Health & Human Services.

Mr. MEEHAN. I think my time is expired. Thank you, Mr. Chairman.

Chairman MCCAUL. I thank the gentleman. I appreciate the point that these "navigators," that navigate people, the American people, through this system, this website, don't undergo a background check. So the idea that convicted felons could be responsible for this is just unconscionable.

With that, the Chairman now recognizes Ms. Sanchez, from California.

Ms. SANCHEZ. Thank you, Mr. Chairman. Thank you, ladies, for being before us today and trying to shed some light on what I believe is an important topic. We need to ensure that we safeguard the information of Americans. So I appreciate the work that you do. When I look at everything that is under your directorates, et cetera it is pretty amazing.

So I have a question. I am trying to come from a more general standpoint because, in a lot of ways, I am a layperson to the technical issues of securing somebody's identity, et cetera. But can you tell us, in general, across the Government networks that we have, what type of operational, administrative, technical, and physical safeguards are implemented to ensure confidentiality, integrity, and availability of PII and to prevent unauthorized or inappropriate access, use, or disclosure of PII?

How does that compare to, for example, HIPAA security standards in place that protect the electronic health information that we have from a medical standpoint?

Ms. STEMPFLEY. Thank you. I appreciate the opportunity. I am personally not familiar with HIPAA in great detail, so I will——

Ms. SANCHEZ. Well, it is one of our standards that we try, supposedly, to uphold so that people don't figure out——

Ms. STEMPFLEY. Absolutely.

Ms. SANCHEZ [continuing]. What has been going on with——

Ms. STEMPFLEY. I am happy to talk about the kinds of administrative procedurals and technical controls that are part of the Federal enterprise security——

Ms. SANCHEZ. Super. In layman's terms, please.

Ms. STEMPFLEY. I will do my best. So one of the most foundational things that is necessary for a viable security program is a set of operational processes and operational responsibility assignments and policy activities. Including things such as ensuring that all users receive annual training for their individual security awareness as a part of their receiving their log-in. That log-ins and passwords are effective. For example, we are in the process of migrating to two-factor authentication, that is a PIV card for log-in.

So it is something more than just your password. You have to have something and know something in order to gain access. As well as the employment of procedures for understanding where your system—what systems you have, where they are, what assets are—what pieces of software are running on them. Then we have been on a long engagement under the Comprehensive National Cyber Security Initiative to create defendable boundaries around the Federal enterprise and to put in place a series of capabilities at those boundaries for better protection and defense.

If you think about it in terms of a community, it is becoming a gated community and one that is focused on securing. You have a set of activities that have to happen for the individuals in the homes, for the homes themselves, and then for the community as a whole. That is a good allegory for laymen, you know, in layman's terms for the kinds of efforts that departments and agencies have to undertake in order to secure their systems and the broad networks that all these activities operate on.

It includes—and I am actually very grateful to this committee and the Members on it for their commitment to capabilities such as the continuous diagnostics and mitigation effort, which we began more than a year ago and are in the process of releasing the contract for providing specific tools and capabilities for departments and agencies to put on their systems and assets. HHS has agreed to be an early adopter of such a capability to include intrusion detection and preventing capabilities that are provided at that boundary level.

Ms. SANCHEZ. Great. I guess I would just say, you know, I always figure, on this committee, when we are looking at cybersecurity in particular, that the weakest link is an individual. So we can protect as much as we want, but, you know, it is what is going on. I remember a few years ago, when our system here within the House was being hacked. It turned out that it was because Members were taking their personal devices overseas and they were being hacked.

So one of the rules we put in was that you either don't take your personal device, you switch out to a dumb device to get some of your e-mails. Or when you land you take out your battery, you know, from your thing, et cetera. Of course, my staff had dumbed me down on my device when I landed, but I saw all my other colleagues turning on their devices. I said, "Oh, do you have a dumb device?" They didn't even understand the policy.

I looked at them, and I said, "You guys, you know the new policy is take out your battery and you can't use your BlackBerry here because, you know, they are getting into our system here." They all looked at me and said, "Oh," they said, "we weren't aware of that policy." I said, "Well, yes, it is a policy because Frank Wolf and others have, you know, they have gotten into our system." To which case they all turned around and started looking at their e-mails.

Chairman MCCAUL. [Off mike.]

Ms. SANCHEZ. So—no, it is true, Mr. Chairman. The other day I was flying back to California. I am on a plane, a colleague—for some reason, my PDA dropped someplace. One of my colleagues picked it up. She said to me, "Oh, you know, I was gonna take a look." I said, "Well, I am password-protected." She looked at me, and I said, "Well, aren't you password-protected on your device?" She looked at me and she goes, "No, it would slow me down."

So we can, you know, we try, and do try. Thank you for the work that you do is, I guess, what I am saying.

Thank you, Mr. Chairman.

Chairman MCCAUL. Thank you.

The Chairman now recognizes the gentleman from South Carolina, Mr. Duncan.

Mr. DUNCAN. Thank you, Mr. Chairman. I am proud to participate in No Shave November to raise awareness of men's health, specifically prostate cancer and cancer in general. I do so in honor and memory of the late South Carolina State representative, my good friend, David Umphlett, who passed away in 2011.

Mr. Chairman, it is crystal clear to me that the Obama administration has put politics over the security of Americans' personal information. President Obama and Secretary Sibelius and other senior officials accepted an excessive amount of risk to Americans' information, all so this flawed website could go forward to meet the Democrats' political agenda.

I have a memo from September 3, 2013, less than a month before the launch of the *HealthCare.gov* website from chief information officer of the Center of Medicare and Medicaid Services, Tony Trenkle. I would like to enter this into the record.

Chairman MCCAUL. Without objection, so ordered.

[The information follows:]

DEPARTMENT OF HEALTH & HUMAN SERVICES •
Centers for Medicare & Medicaid Services
7500 Security Boulevard, Mail Stop N3-15-25
Baltimore, Maryland 21244-1850

OFFICE OF INFORMATION SERVICES

CENTERS FOR MEDICARE & MEDICAID SERVICES
MEMORANDUM

DATE: SEP 3 2013

TO: Director,
Consortium for Medicare Health Plans Operations (OA/CMHPO) and Acting
Deputy Center Director for Operations, Center for Consumer Information and
Insurance Oversight (CCIIO)

FROM: Chief Information Officer and
Director, Office of Information Services (OIS)

SUBJECT: Authorization Decision for the Federal Facilitated Marketplaces (FFM) System

ACTION REQUIRED 30 DAYS FROM THE DATE OF THIS MEMORANDUM

The Federal Facilitated Marketplaces (FFM) System is a *Moderate* level system located at the
Terremark Datacenter in Culpeper, Virginia. The system maintains records used to support all
Health Insurance Exchange Programs established by the Centers for Medicare & Medicaid
Services (CMS) under the health care reform provisions of the Affordable Care Act (Public Law
11-148). FFM will help qualified individuals and small business employers shop for, select, and
pay for high-quality, affordable health coverage. Exchanges will have the capability to
determine eligibility for coverage through the Exchange, for tax credits and cost-sharing
reductions, and for Medicaid, Basic Health Plan (BHP) and Children's Health Insurance Program
(CHIP) coverage. As part of the eligibility and enrollment process, financial, demographic, and
(potentially) health information will flow through the Exchange.

On August 8, 2013, you certified the controls for the system and submitted along with your
certification the other required documentation necessary to obtain an Authorization to Operate
(ATO) for FFM.

I have determined through a thorough review of the authorization package that the risk to CMS
information and information systems resulting from the operation of the FFM information
system is acceptable predicated on the completion of the actions described in the attachment.
Accordingly, **I am issuing an Authorization to Operate (ATO)** for the FFM information
system to operate in its current environment and configuration until **August 31, 2014.** The
current configuration includes only the Federal Facilitated Marketplaces Qualified Health Plans
(QHP) and Dental modules. This system is not authorized to establish any new connections or
interfaces with non-CMS FISMA or other non-CMS connections without prior approval during
the period of this ATO. An impact analysis must be conducted for any system changes
implemented after the issuance of this ATO. Any major modifications that affect the security
posture of the system will require an appropriately scoped security controls assessment and
issuance of a new ATO.

CGIHR00002826

The security authorization of the information system will remain in effect until the indicated expiration date if the following conditions are maintained:

(i) Required periodic security status reports for the system are submitted to this office in accordance with current CMS policy;

(ii) New vulnerabilities reported during the continuous monitoring process do not result in additional agency-level risk that is deemed unacceptable; and

(iii) The system has not exceeded the maximum allowable time between security authorizations in accordance with Federal or CMS policy.

The attachment provides information on requirements not met, as well as corrective actions needed to bring them into compliance. The actions set forth in the attachment must be entered into the approved CMS Plan of Action and Milestones (POA&M) tracking tool no later than 30 days from the date of this memorandum, and the action items addressed no later than the designated completion dates. This office will monitor all POA&M items submitted during the period of authorization.

If you have questions, please contact Teresa Fryer, Chief Information Security Officer (CISO), at ████████. The DISPC team is also available to support staff level questions at ████@cms.hhs.gov.

Tony Trenkle

Attachment

cc:
Mark Oh, Director OIS/CIISG/DHIM
Darrin Lyles, ISSO, OIS/CIISG/DSMDS
Teresa Fryer, CISO, Director OIS/EISG
Michael Mellor, Dep. CISO, Dep. Director OIS/EISG
Desmond Young, OIS/EISG/DISPC
Jessica Hoffman, OIS/EISG/DISPC
James Mensah, OIS/EISG/DISPC

CGIHR00002827

29

Attachment

Federally Facilitated Marketplaces (FFM) System

Authorization Decision

Authorization decision is required for the following reason(s):

X	New System
	Major system modification
	Serious security violation
	Changes in the threat environment
	Expired authorization to operate

I. Authorization Decision

I have reviewed the information concerning the request for an Authorization to Operate and with consideration of the recommendations provided by my staff; I concur with the assessment of the security risk. This risk has been weighed against the business operational requirements and security measures that have or will be implemented. I have determined the following authorization decision is appropriate.

X	**Authorization to Operate** The current risk is deemed acceptable. The applicable system is authorized to operate until the designated date, subject to the authorization actions in Section II.

This authorization will expire: August 31, 2014. This authorization may be withdrawn at the discretion of the Authorizing Official for lack of progress on the authorization actions in Section II, or any security violations deemed to increase the risk to CMS beyond a tolerable level.

	Denial of Authorization to Operate The current risk is deemed unacceptable. The applicable system may not operate until the authorization actions listed in Section II are completed, after which, verification of corrective actions and resubmission of the authorization package is required.

(Authorizing Official Signature and Date)
Tony Trenkle
CMS Chief Information Officer

Attachment

Federally Facilitated Marketplaces (FFM) System

II. Authorization Actions

Failure to meet the assigned due dates without prior approval invalidates this authorization to operate. The following specific actions are to be completed by the date(s) indicated:

Finding	Finding Description	Recommended Corrective Action	Risk	Due Date
FFM has an open high finding:	the threat and risk potential is limitless.		The presence of high risk findings in a system represents an increased risk to the CMS enterprise. Lifecycle management of the system requires initial testing for FISMA authorization and continuous monitoring. Non-compliance with the *CMS Information Security (IS) Acceptable Risk Safeguards (ARS), CMS Minimum Security Requirements (CMSR)* without continuous monitoring presents an unacceptable risk. (CA-2).	May 31, 2014

CGIHR00002829

Attachment

Federally Facilitated Marketplaces (FFM) System

Finding	Finding Description	Recommended Corrective Action	Risk	Due Date
FFM has an open high finding: ▮▮▮	▮▮▮▮▮	▮▮▮▮▮ ▮▮▮▮▮	The presence of high risk findings in a system represents an increased risk to the CMS enterprise. Lifecycle management of the system requires initial testing for FISMA authorization and continuous monitoring. Non-compliance with the *CMS Information Security (IS) Acceptable Risk Safeguards (ARS), CMS Minimum Security Requirements (CMSR)* without continuous monitoring presents an unacceptable risk. (CA-2).	February 26, 2015

CGIHR00002830

Federally Facilitated Marketplaces (FFM) System

Finding	Finding Description	Recommended Corrective Action	Risk	Due Date
■	Security controls are not documented as being fully implemented.	■	There is the possibility that the FFM security controls are ineffective. Ineffective controls do not appropriately protect the confidentiality, integrity and availability of data and present a risk to the CMS enterprise. (PL-2).	February 7, 2014
■	■	■	■ ...exposes the enterprise to additional risk. (RA-2).	February 7, 2014
■	■	Review the FIPS 199 inheritance selections in CFACTS and either select the appropriate inheritance or indicate the controls are solely the responsibility of FFM.	■ can lead to controls not being appropriately implemented and a lack of accountability. ■	February 7, 2014

Attachment

Federally Facilitated Marketplaces (FFM) System

Finding	Finding Description	Recommended Corrective Action	Risk	Due Date
Inconsistent Points of Contact (POCs).	The system developer/maintainer on the CMS Security Certification Form is a different person from ███	Identify and update the appropriate system POCs for all of the documents and provide the updated POCs ████	Unclear role responsibility can affect the life cycle support of the system. ███	February 7, 2014

END OF ACTIONS

Mr. DUNCAN. Thank you. Approving authorization to operate the system underlying the Obamacare health exchanges. Trenkle states the risk to CMS information systems resulting from the operation of the FFM, or Obamacare—FFM stands for Federal Facilitated Marketplaces—information systems is acceptable. But the memo then goes on to say page after page, describing enormous risk to Americans' personal information. Page 2 discusses, "malicious macros, the threat and risk potential is limitless."

Page 3: "No evidence of functional testing processes and procedures being adequate to identify functional problems resulting in non-functional code being deployed." Page 4: "Many FFM controls documented in the security controls section of CFACS have an effectiveness of not satisfied. Security controls are not documented as being fully implemented." It goes on: "Ineffective controls do not appropriately protect the confidentiality, integrity, and availability of data, and present a risk to the CMS enterprise."

These show serious concerns in the security of the Obamacare exchanges. It makes clear that Obamacare represents a clear and present danger to Americans' personal information. How could anyone with a technology background assess that with all this that the risk was acceptable to move forward? Which they did, and launched a website October 1. Why weren't security officials in DHS and HHS and others sounding the alarm about the concerns raised by Mr. Trenkle? Is it in any way conceivable that these issues could be solved by the end of this month?

That is a rhetorical question. We may get back with any conclusion. Mr. Chairman, I find it quite convenient that, in 2 days, Mr. Trenkle has decided to cut and run from HHS and go into the private sector; not to be accountable to the oversight functions of Congress anymore. The American people deserve accountability for the threat this administration has allowed to our personal information.

I would like to also share an article from South Carolina, a Columbia, South Carolina gentleman, an attorney. Went onto the *HealthCare.gov* website to browse for cheaper insurance for him and his wife. He entered in his information, just as you would normally do. A few days later, he had someone call him from North Carolina. He says, "I believe, somehow, the ACA health care website has sent me your information. That is what it looks like to me," Mr. Judson Hadley said, a North Carolina resident, who could access Tom's information on *HealthCare.gov*.

I think there is a problem with the wrong information going to the wrong place. Now, the article goes on to say that Mr. Hadley just entered into the website to try to shop for insurance for himself and he was sent this gentleman from South Carolina's personal information. He actually went to another link and clicked on it, and actually had a PDF that he could print out on his computer of all of this gentleman's information. These are serious flaws.

This wasn't a hacker, this wasn't someone trying to intentionally access Americans' private information. This was information sent to a third party by *HealthCare.gov*. This website has serious problems. Americans are relying on this Government to get it right. So I go back to the question that I had asked rhetorically a minute ago: Is it any way conceivable these issues could be solved, Ms. Stempfley, by the end of this month?

Ms. STEMPFLEY. Again, sir, I respectfully submit that that question is best asked to the Department of Health & Human Services.

Mr. DUNCAN. Are you aware of Mr. Trenkle's memo? Have you seen that?

Ms. STEMPFLEY. I believe I saw that this morning, sir.

Mr. DUNCAN. Okay. Well, it will be entered into the record.

Mr. Chairman, thank you for having this hearing. Americans expect us to get it right. If not, let's delay Obamacare implementation until the Government can assure Americans that their private information will not be stolen by a third party and their identity be taken that could cause serious financial harm to them and their families.

With that, I yield back.

Chairman MCCAUL. I thank the gentleman for his insight.

The Chairman now recognizes the gentleman from New Jersey, Mr. Payne.

Mr. PAYNE. Thank you, Mr. Chairman. Ms. Stempfley and Ms. Correa, I appreciate your being here today and your testimony. From my understanding, the Federal data service hub is not a database or a repository for personally identifying information or for health care records in general. Is that correct?

Ms. STEMPFLEY. Sir, I am not personally familiar with the architecture of *HealthCare.gov*.

Mr. PAYNE. Ms. Correa.

Ms. CORREA. I am not familiar with their—I don't know exactly what their architecture is. My understanding, it is not. It is just a conduit for passing information.

Mr. PAYNE. That is my understanding, as well. I think that needs to be clarified. You know, again, from my understanding, this hub will just be used to determine someone's eligibility to participate in the exchange, enroll in a plan, receive a tax credit, and determine whether someone is entitled to an exemption only. Is that your understanding?

Ms. CORREA. From the accounts that I have read, yes, that is my understanding. That it is a help to process information.

Mr. PAYNE. Okay. Let's see. Can you describe how the Federal agencies like HHS, DHS, the IRS, and Social Security Administration are coordinating with one another and with insurance carriers to share information, and how is that information being protected?

Ms. CORREA. I can speak to the agreements that we enter into—"we," as in USCIS enter into—with our partner agencies who have the databases that we go out and look at. We enter into some form of an agreement, either a memorandum of agreement or a computer matching agreement—that is the agreement that we entered into with HHS—and we also have what are called "service-level" agreements. Service-level agreements typically talk about performance in terms of when we go out and query a database what kind of response times we can expect.

So those are the kinds of agreements that we enter into. Again, I do want to emphasize that our SAVE program doesn't download information from those databases. We merely go out, ping those databases for information, obtain the immigration status and the class of admission, and provide that information back to the inquiring agency.

Mr. PAYNE. Okay. It is—you know, it—do Federal agencies often share personal identifiable information for the purposes like processing Social Security claims? How is that information protected? You know, is the same approach being used for those enrolling in these exchanges?

Ms. STEMPFLEY. Sir, unfortunately, it is atypical for the Department to engage at a system level in that perspective. Although one of the requirements under—for example, under FISMA, is an interconnection agreement which is put in place between two systems that are—articulates the security requirements that both parties must be subject to.

Mr. PAYNE. Okay. One last question. You know, as you ladies know, the changes are being made to *HealthCare.gov* to make it run better. What steps are being taken in coordination with these changes to ensure that personally identifiable information is still protected?

Ms. STEMPFLEY. Sir, again, I think, respectfully, that question is best directed to the Department of Health & Human Services.

Mr. PAYNE. Okay. Well, with that, Mr. Chairman, I will yield back.

Chairman McCAUL. The Chairman will now recognize the gentleman from Pennsylvania, Mr. Perry.

Mr. PERRY. Thank you, Mr. Chairman. Thank you, ladies, for being here. Just looking for your overall assessment, because I think we—at least I, as a Member, and I think many of my constituents, members of Citizens of America—are concerned, wondering who is responsible. So I am looking for your broad knowledge of the system. To where does an American whose information has been compromised, to whom does that person seek redress?

Is there an individual, is there an agency? What is the mechanism to be made whole once your information is compromised and who knows what it is used for? If there someone that you know of, is there any agency? Where do Americans go when it goes bad, if it goes bad?

Ms. STEMPFLEY. As a normal—sort of in the normal course of events across the Federal enterprise, if a citizen experiences an issue with a Federal application, typically the first place they go is that application's support desk or support function. That is generally escalated to security operation centers inside the organization, and then further escalated to the Department of Homeland Security for visibility and for response functions.

Mr. PERRY. So it would be the Homeland Security—it would be the——

Ms. STEMPFLEY. Department of Health & Human Services. Generally, it is the support function for whatever that application might be.

Mr. PERRY. Would they be able to seek financial remuneration for, you know, some kind of grievance? Or if their identity was taken and their accounts were emptied and their lives were destroyed from a digital standpoint would they be—is that where they would go?

Ms. STEMPFLEY. I am sorry, sir, that is not an area of expertise of mine about—in the redress areas. I will be happy to take the question——

Mr. PERRY. Okay, appreciate it. Ms. Correa, do you know? Okay.

Ms. CORREA. I do not.

Mr. PERRY. Ms. Correa, I appreciate you being here. It provides a unique opportunity. If you can explain CIS's role in identifying somebody who comes here illegally to access our services and tries to sign up on the exchange, what is the role there of CIS in identifying that person? What is the process?

Ms. CORREA. Thank you for your question and the opportunity to clarify how the process works. The benefit-granting agency is the organization that determines the eligibility of whether an individual is eligible for a particular benefit. They come to us through the—in this case, the Affordable Care Act, through the hub. They come to us, they provide us with information such as their alien number, their I–94 number, their name, their date of birth, et cetera. That is the data that we use to go out and verify the immigration status of the individual.

The SAVE responds with the immigration status information as well as the class of administration—if it is able to confirm the immigration status based on the information presented. However, any decision on the eligibility for benefits is made at the benefit-granting agency level. In other words, USCIS does not make that determination.

Mr. PERRY. Okay. Do you know, if you can tell me, how long that process takes? I am looking, just so you understand, in the context of the administration has on numerous occasions said that the process should take about 25 minutes to sign up. So all that, in my mind, has to occur, right, before you can sign up? This is all in the span of 25 minutes. Is that—do you have any idea of the time that that process takes?

Ms. CORREA. I would like to clarify that the sign-up process is happening outside of this SAVE process. That sign-up process is before the exchange comes through the hub, to us, for a SAVE query. So I wouldn't know how long that process would take. What I can share with you is our response times, as I mentioned, in our testimony. From the moment we receive a query, either in the initial verification step or in the subsequent steps, how long that takes. But I couldn't talk about how long does it really take to sign up.

Mr. PERRY. Just for the record, again, what is your time frame?

Ms. CORREA. Sure. Our average response time in the initial query is about 3 to 5 seconds. On the ACA, right now, the queries that we are getting through we are seeing about 1.31 seconds response times.

Mr. PERRY. Okay.

Ms. CORREA. For the second step, it takes about 3 to 5 Federal working days. For the third step, which is the more complex steps, it takes about 10 to 20 Federal working days.

Mr. PERRY. Okay. So is that—am I to take it to mean as far as you can tell that somebody that is here illegally that maybe came just to sign up for benefits could do that, and be involved in—could go through the exchange and sign up for benefits, and receive a plan, before they could be identified as being here illegally?

Ms. CORREA. Let me clarify that someone who is here illegally, who is undocumented——

Mr. PERRY. Right.

Ms. CORREA [continuing]. Is not likely to be able to come through the hub with a query. Because the benefit-granting agency, when an individual attests that they are either not a U.S. citizen or—if an individual attests that they are not a U.S. citizen they have to present their documentation as to what their status is.

Mr. PERRY. Right.

Ms. CORREA. That is the information that the benefit-granting agency would enter into the system—or the individual would have to enter that information if they are entering directly—to come through for a query. So an undocumented individual wouldn't have that information and wouldn't be able to be the subject of a query.

Mr. PERRY. Thank you. I see my time is expired, and I yield back.

Chairman MCCAUL. I thank the gentleman.

Mr. Duncan referred to an article during his questioning that he would like to make part of the record. I would like to ask unanimous consent that it be made a part of the record.

Ms. JACKSON LEE. Will the gentleman yield?

Chairman MCCAUL. The Chairman yields to the gentlelady.

Ms. JACKSON LEE. I am sorry. I did not hear what the document was. Would you just repeat for the record what the document was?

Chairman MCCAUL. It had to deal with a gentleman from, I believe, North Carolina that tried to sign up for Obamacare and got information back regarding another gentleman from South Carolina, very personal information, that has been widely reported.

Ms. JACKSON LEE. So it is a newspaper article?

Chairman MCCAUL. Correct.

Ms. JACKSON LEE. I thank the gentleman. I yield.

Chairman MCCAUL. Okay. Without objection, so ordered.

[The information follows:]

ARTICLE SUBMITTED FOR THE RECORD BY HON. JEFF DUNCAN

MIDLANDS MAN HAS PERSONAL INFORMATION COMPROMISED ON HEALTHCARE.GOV

Posted: Nov 03, 2013 6:22 PM EST

Updated: Nov 04, 2013 4:04 PM EST

By Meaghan Norman

COLUMBIA, SC (WIS).—About a month ago, attorney Tom Dougall logged on to healthcare.gov to browse for cheaper insurance for him and his wife.

On Friday, the last thing he expected to hear on his voicemail was a man from North Carolina who says he can access all of Tom's personal information.

Dougall says he thought it was a scam until he realized his privacy had been breached.

"I believe somehow the ACA, the Healthcare website has sent me your information, is what it looks like," said Justin Hadley, a North Carolina resident who could access Tom's information on healthcare.gov. "I think there's a problem with the wrong information getting to the wrong people."

In a telephone interview, Hadley said he simply put in his username and password when Dougall's information appeared.

"The next page that came up was a page that prompted that I have a marketplace eligibility information to download. And that's when I clicked download and Mr. Dougall's information came up in a PDF document," said Hadley.

At first, Dougall didn't know what to think.

"We received a phone call from a gentleman named Justin in North Carolina who informed me that he had gone on the healthcare.gov website and when he logged in under his log in and password, he received a document of all of my and my wife's personal information," Dougall said.

Dougall said he thought it was a ploy.

"Initially I was concerned because I didn't know if this was some guy who was scamming me or if in fact this was a guy who really had my personal information," he said.

Hadley even provided proof, documents containing Tom's personal information and screen shots of the website.

"And you can see that he's actually signed in as Justin and it tells him he has notices about his marketplace eligibility and to download those and when he downloads it, the next screen shot shows him my personal information," Dougall said.

Dougall said now Hadley cannot sign up for the coverage he needs because he's been blocked by Tom's personal information.

"I'm assuming I'm going to have to pay the penalty or tax or whatever they're calling it now for not having health insurance next year," said Hadley.

"We're told constantly that it's a secure system and it's not, obviously," Dougall said.

Having lived through one security breach in the State of South Carolina with the Department of Revenue, Dougall wonders what would happen if a professional hacker tried to log on.

"I tried to call healthcare.gov last night and they have no procedure whatsoever to handle security breaches," he said. "All they can do is try to sell you a policy."

Dougall has also contacted his Congressmen. He says he's calling the Department of Health and Human Services directly on Monday.

"They're so concerned with trying to fix the problems they currently have that they refuse to acknowledge or won't acknowledge that there's been a major breach," Dougall said.

In the mean time, Dougall does not know how to secure his information.

"I think there's a problem with the wrong information getting to the wrong people," Dougall said.

We reached out the U.S. Department of Health and Human Services, they responded via email Sunday afternoon asking for more information about what happened to Tom and Justin.

Late Sunday, an HHS official said a security team is working to fix the issue. "We are aware of this issue and it is on our punch list of fixes, scheduled to be addressed in the very near future."

They added consumers can call the toll-free number or access the on-line chat tool that is available 24/7.

Chairman McCAUL. The Chairman now recognizes the gentleman from Texas, Mr. O'Rourke.

Mr. O'ROURKE. Thank you, Mr. Chairman. Thank you for holding this hearing.

The implementation of the Affordable Care Act, thus far, has been deeply disappointing. Most obviously, the roll-out of the website has been a disaster. I want to work to make sure that we fix those problems that we have identified. I want to make sure that we make this law work. It is, after all, the law of the land. It has been tested several times, and tested at the level of the Supreme Court. The Government was effectively shut down, in part, in dispute and debate over this.

I think politically, legislatively, that has been resolved. Now we need to make sure that it works. Again, the implementation so far has been disappointing. But I want to work with Members from both sides to fix those problems that we have identified, and there are many, and make this work.

I think about the 200,000 El Pasoans that I represent who are currently uninsured. Who, because of their lack of insurance, are gonna have worse health outcomes than they otherwise would. Who, because they don't have insurance, when they do get care, the rest of us are subsidizing that care in a very ineffective, inefficient, and costly manner.

So I want to make sure that this law works. I think its goals and intentions are noble. I think it is perfectable. So I want to make sure that we are focused on that. In today's hearing, we are looking at cybersecurity threats and problems. Some of the questions resolved around—or revolved around a tax on *HealthCare.gov*. Denial of service attacks, hacking attempts, attempts to gain access, or entry, illegally.

I am assuming, and correct me if I am wrong, that every single Government web asset is attacked, perhaps on a daily or a minute-by-minute basis. Is that correct?

Ms. STEMPFLEY. Certainly, sir. The internet itself, where we operate in this environment, is one that contains a multitude of threats. The Federal Government websites and Federal Government systems are subject to the same environment and these same threats.

Mr. O'ROURKE. So the existence of threats, proof that attacks have taken place, do not prove the system is vulnerable. Or, from your answer to the previous question from the Chairman, do not establish that you have concerns about the security of that system. Is that correct?

Ms. STEMPFLEY. Certainly, sir. The existence of threats does not increase the vulnerability that the systems might be——

Mr. O'ROURKE. Have you seen anything, thus far—you know, a month-and-a-half in—that would give you concern about threats that might be realized, or vulnerabilities that might be exploited that have not been addressed so far by the administration or HHS?

Ms. STEMPFLEY. The position that the Department of Homeland Security exists is in both awareness and in reporting has only provided limited information, at this point. As I said earlier, we received about 16 reports from HHS that are under investigation, and one open-source report about a denial of service.

Mr. O'ROURKE. In thinking about the VA, and the fact that the VA is trying to move to a much more web- and digital-based sharing of service records and medical records for former servicemembers, anything that we can learn from the success or failures in those VA programs that are sharing very sensitive information? In some case, I realize that information has been compromised. Anything we can learn, or what lessons have we learned, that we are able to apply to what we are doing now with *HealthCare.gov*?

Ms. STEMPFLEY. So I believe I mentioned that the HHS CIO as well as the VA CIO are members of the CIO council and of the CISO forums. Those are—the CISO forum specifically is one that we in DHS run to ensure that we have an avenue for that sharing of current activity and lessons learned in engagement. There is a series of best practice documents and actions that are published by DHS that are an amalgamation of all of that learning and that are available.

Mr. O'ROURKE. Do you know, specifically, if the VA has shared that information from their best practices and what they have learned from failures within that system?

Ms. STEMPFLEY. I could not speak to a VA-to-HHS-specific conversation. But we have the aggregation of all of those in a published format so the departments and agencies can gain access to that around the clock.

Mr. O'ROURKE. Ms. Correa, let me ask you a question. In El Paso, there are bound to be many mixed-status families amongst those 200,000 uninsured people that I represent in our community. Walk me through what happens when you have a U.S. citizen child to a parent who has undocumented status currently. How will they use that system? How will you use that information if you learn that that parent is here in an undocumented fashion?

Ms. CORREA. As I mentioned before—thank you for your question, but as I mentioned before, what we would see is the information about that child that they are applying for a particular benefit. So the benefit-granting agency would be entering that information. That is the only information that we would be processing through the query. If the undocumented parent were trying to apply for a benefit, if they don't have documentation, then we wouldn't see that query because there would be no information to enter into the system.

Mr. O'ROURKE. With the Chairman's indulgence, if I could just ask a quick question.

Ms. CORREA. Sure——

Mr. O'ROURKE. If you somehow through this system, *HealthCare.gov*, learn that the parent is here illegally, would you act on that information, and how would you act on that information?

Ms. CORREA. I would like to confirm my answer on this, but we do not rely on that information. Because, again, we only see a fragment of data. So there is nothing that we would do with that information at this time.

Mr. O'ROURKE. Okay, thank you.

Thank you, Mr. Chairman.

Chairman MCCAUL. Gentleman.

The gentlelady from Michigan, Mrs. Miller, is recognized.

Mrs. MILLER. Thank you, Mr. Chairman. I certainly thank you for calling this very important hearing on this issue.

My question to the two of you—and I appreciate your attendance here today—as I have listened to the questions from my other colleagues, it is certainly clear from your answers and your testimony that the Department of Homeland Security has not been intimately involved in protecting the security of the most personal and most private information of American citizens through the *HealthCare.gov* website. That that responsibility rests, as you kept testifying, solely—at this point, solely with the Department of Health & Human Services. Many times, you said that question should be asked of them, not of you.

So my question to you, then, would be: Do you play a role in determining acceptable risk when the Department of Homeland Security—not the other departments or the Department of HHS, but the Department of Homeland Security—do you play a role in determining what is acceptable risk when the Department of Homeland Security launches—when you launch, that—your department launches a new website within the Department? Mr. Duncan was reading off a list of serious risks that the HHS had identified before the launch of the *HealthCare.gov*.

If the Department of Homeland Security would have identified those kinds of risks, similar risks, before you launched a website for the DHS—not one of the other departments, your department—would you have found that risk acceptable, and would you have advocated the launch of that website?

Ms. STEMPFLEY. In the Department of Homeland Security, the right principle risk acceptance official is the chief information officer, and that is an organization roughly parallel to mine. We have a strong engagement with the chief information officer through a series of information exchanges. It is not typical, even in the Department of Homeland Security, for that risk official to reach out to us on specific systems or applications as they go forward. We engage with them through the same broad conversations as we go forward.

For the information technology systems that we operate as I pointed out, things like the continuous diagnostics and mitigation program and the intrusion detection programs like EINSTEIN, which I am grateful to this committee for its support of—we are responsive to the CIO in detailing the compliance actions forward and ensuring compliance with security standards that are set. So there is a——

Mrs. MILLER. But would you have raised any question at all? I mean, I understand you don't want to answer any questions about HHS. But now you can't even answer a question about your own Department. Although you say typically you talk back and forth, typically——

Ms. STEMPFLEY. For——

Mrs. MILLER. I mean, typically you can't even raise a red flag?

Ms. STEMPFLEY. For the magnitude of the numbers of applications that we are talking about, ma'am, are substantial. For example, in HHS, in their FISMA 2012 report, they reported 10,648 individual applications. So within any specific one it is difficult to go in great detail. For the application——

Mrs. MILLER. So typically, since I have a limited amount of time—typically you can't even raise those questions, right? Typically?

Ms. STEMPFLEY. Typically, under the current authority and landscape, that is a true statement.

Mrs. MILLER. Okay. Well, that is an interesting answer. I appreciate your candor. You can't raise a question if you have those kinds of problems. Could you, then—shifting gears just for a moment, I wanted to pick on something the Chairman mentioned at the outset. Typically, the Congress has oversight responsibilities. Typically, when we have hearings like this, typically—for hundreds of years, typically we get testimony from the witnesses typically at a deadline.

Now in this case, for whatever reason, we did not get—whether you were unwilling or unable to give us your testimony. I mean, as a Member of Congress, trying to typically do my job, I am trying to read the information the day before, the night before, whatever so that I can be prepared, typically. But in this case, we couldn't get your testimony before the hearing. Now, I don't know if that is typical for you or your Department not to respond on the deadline. Usually we do get it.

The Chairman mentioned perhaps it is because the White House wouldn't allow you, in this case, to give us the information. Could you expand for me, at least, why that was—you were not able, you were unable or unwilling, to give us your testimony to meet the deadline which is a typical situation?

Ms. STEMPFLEY. It certainly is—I am a believer of being prepared myself, and so it is certainly a goal of all of ours to ensure that we provide information in as rapid a manner as possible to individuals. In my office we work very hard to ensure that we are responsive and within the controls and constraints that we operate under. So I am pleased that you were willing to have us here to speak, even though the testimony did not arrive to you in time. So thank you for that.

I am not familiar with all of the steps between here and arriving on your door to speak to this specific event. I am happy to go back and get you an answer.

Mrs. MILLER. Thank you. Mr. Chairman, we are apparently not going to get any answers out of these witnesses, so I appreciate that. Appreciate the time. Thank you.

Chairman MCCAUL. I appreciate the gentlelady's questioning. I—as the Chairman of this committee, I would like to know, did you prepare an opening statement?

Ms. STEMPFLEY. Yes, sir.

Chairman MCCAUL. That opening statement was not delivered to this committee. Is that correct?

Ms. STEMPFLEY. I believe I—you mean an oral statement or a written statement?

Chairman MCCAUL. We—well, we did not have your written opening statement.

Ms. STEMPFLEY. I believe that——

Chairman MCCAUL. Until 9 o'clock this morning.

Ms. STEMPFLEY. Yes, until this morning. I believe that is a true statement—5 copies——

Chairman MCCAUL. So it was held up by somebody, correct?

Ms. STEMPFLEY. Again, sir, I——

Chairman MCCAUL. I see you have to refer to counsel. But can you tell the Chairman?

Ms. STEMPFLEY. There is a process for——

Chairman MCCAUL. Of course there is. But when did you finish your draft of your opening statement?

Ms. STEMPFLEY. Thursday? Thursday?

Chairman MCCAUL. So Thursday, and here we are today——

Ms. STEMPFLEY. Yes, sir.

Chairman MCCAUL [continuing]. You know, many days later. Who approved your statement?

Ms. STEMPFLEY. Who approved my statement?

Chairman MCCAUL. Correct.

Ms. STEMPFLEY. It goes through a series of—the gentleman who understands the process better than I do. I submit it to the Department, and the Department submits it forward.

Chairman MCCAUL. Okay.

Ms. STEMPFLEY. I am not sure—I don't have a name of who approved it.

Chairman MCCAUL. You do not know who held up your statement.

Ms. STEMPFLEY. I don't know, sir.

Chairman MCCAUL. Okay. I would like to know who did, and why. Because as Mrs. Miller stated, this is not typical.

Ms. STEMPFLEY. I understand.

Chairman MCCAUL. In fact, extraordinary. I personally think it is due to the sensitivity of this issue. I would like to know whether the White House did hold this statement up.

With that, the Chairman now recognizes the gentleman from Nevada, Mr. Horsford.

Mr. HORSFORD. Thank you, Mr. Chairman. I will try to be brief. I want to fist associate myself with the comments of the Ranking Member and several other Members of the committee who, like myself listening to my constituents, am concerned about where things stand with the roll-out of the Affordable Care Act website and the ability for my constituents and constituents across the country to effectively access and shop for plans that are available. Fortunately, in the State of Nevada, our Governor, despite being opposed to the law, worked with the legislature to implement a State exchange.

So we are better off than many States that have—continuing to oppose the implementation of the laws, as required. I am a bit perplexed by some of the comments that have been made this morning by my colleagues on the other side that are so outraged by the glitches and the fact that there are security concerns with *HealthCare.gov.* Particularly because, as a Member of the Subcommittee on Cybersecurity, Infrastructure Protection, and Security Technologies, we have had many, many, many hearings about the vulnerabilities of personal identifiable information in the private sector, as well.

There are financial institutions, there are private health care companies that do not do a good job of protecting that information in the private sector. So if we could just work together, the two sides, to identify those challenges, and work towards solving them in both the public and private sector, then I think the public would be better off. But unfortunately, we have things like the House Republican playbook that helped to disseminate information for how people shouldn't navigate the system effectively and, instead, just bring the negative information forward.

So I want to just ask our panel a couple of questions. First, Ms. Stempfley, thank you very much for being here. I know you have testified several times before the Subcommittee on Cybersecurity, Infrastructure Protection, and Security Technologies before. To the best of your knowledge, are the HIPAA privacy and security standards applicable to the exchanges and the data service hub?

Ms. STEMPFLEY. Sir, as I believe I said, I am not a HIPAA expert. So I would be happy to find one to answer that question for you, but you are certainly on the edges of my personal knowledge.

Mr. HORSFORD. From my understanding, obviously the HIPAA rules as established set Federal standards to protect individually identifiable health information. That is a Federal requirement.

Ms. STEMPFLEY. Yes.

Mr. HORSFORD. Correct?

Ms. STEMPFLEY. Yes.

Mr. HORSFORD. The Department of Homeland Security is required to meet those Federal privacy and security standards, correct?

Ms. STEMPFLEY. As with HHSB, yes, sir.

Mr. HORSFORD. So how do you go about doing that within your Department?

Ms. STEMPFLEY. Forgive me, sir. Can you ask the question one more time?

Mr. HORSFORD. How does the Department of Homeland Security go about ensuring Federal privacy and security standards apply under HIPAA?

Ms. STEMPFLEY. Thank you. Great, thank you. So I—in my office in DHS, we don't actually operate systems who contain that kind of information. So I can speak in general terms about the kinds of requirements we would operate under, and assume that the HIPAA requirements would be similar in that situation. So we are required to submit forward a package of evidence demonstrating our compliance with each of these requirements to the accrediting official.

Then the accrediting official reviews that package of evidence to determine that—to demonstrate that we have, in fact, provided that compliance as they are making their accrediting decision.

Mr. HORSFORD. Does the same apply for immigration?

Ms. CORREA. Yes, sir, that is correct. From a system-owner standpoint, that is the process that we follow. We submit the package of information. It goes to the accreditation official, which normally resides within the chief information officer's office, and they do the accrediting of the system.

Mr. HORSFORD. One last question in my concluding time allowed. The issue around the breach procedures. When there is a breach, what is the requirement in Federal law for the notification of the individual and States if the breach reached a certain number of individuals?

Ms. STEMPFLEY. So, certainly, one of the things that we have been talking about with the subcommittee, sir, is that there is not a single Federal breach require—Federal law associated with data breach requirements. That there is a multitude of State laws that are out there. So I appreciate your raising this issue that I know we have spoken of. When it comes to Federal systems, if personally identifiable information is, in fact—there has been a breach of personally identifiable information, Department and agency leadership are responsible for making a determination of the scope of that breach and for reporting that to the Department of Homeland Security. We also through the annual report forwarded both to OMB and to—and in the FISMA report.

Mr. HORSFORD. Thank you, Mr. Chairman.

Chairman MCCAUL. The Chairman recognizes the gentleman from Utah, Mr. Stewart.

Mr. STEWART. Thank you, Mr. Chairman. I am gonna go quickly. There is a lot I want to cover.

I want to come back to a couple comments that have been made previous, and then—to the witnesses. To Mr. Horsford, I appreciate your comments about trying to work together. I would remind the committee that that is what we were trying to do. That is why we asked the administration for a delay. But the President assured us again and again and again, he promised the American people we are ready. That is why he refused to work with us on any kind of a delay. Of course, we found out now that that is not the case.

I want to come back to—just very quickly, about your opening—not your opening comment, but your opening statements. Did anyone ever advise either of you that they were not going to submit those statements to the committee?

Ms. STEMPFLEY. No, sir. I believe it was the 5th of November when I was asked to speak in front of this committee, and no one has advised that they weren't gonna be provided.

Mr. STEWART. So——

Ms. STEMPFLEY. It was just a number of days between the 5th of November and the——

Mr. STEWART. Okay. So last Thursday you prepared your opening statements. You passed those up the line. No one ever asked you to revise them, no one ever indicated any problems with them. They just disappeared and no one ever saw them, including the committee, until this morning. Is that right?

Ms. STEMPFLEY. Sir, a number of grammatical errors were identified and corrected——

Mr. STEWART. But nothing substantial.

Ms. STEMPFLEY [continuing]. In the course of it. But no, there was no——

Mr. STEWART. They didn't come to you say this is unacceptable, we can't submit this the way it is.

Ms. STEMPFLEY. There was—I am trying to remember what it started and what it looked like when I got it back. But it was effectively—it was written and it was sort of choppy and smoothed out. But there were no changes.

Mr. STEWART. Okay. So as far as you know, your opening statements were acceptable. Okay. But, apparently, someone concluded they were not because they were not submitted to the committee.

Ms. STEMPFLEY. Sir, I would not—respectfully, sir, I believe it was just a matter of between the 5th of November and the 13th of November——

Mr. STEWART. Okay.

Ms. STEMPFLEY [continuing]. Going through the set of processes. It wasn't a——

Mr. STEWART. Well, perhaps. Although I think there may be others who would say that it was more than just that. But let me move on, if I could.

You are both Federal employees, and you both will stay on the Federal Employee Health Benefits program. Is that right? Yes. You are not gonna move to the exchanges. Of course, both of you realize that I will, Members of the committee will, all of our staff will. In fact, tens of millions of Americans are gonna be forced to move onto the exchanges beginning, you know, January 1, where they will be forced, in order to do that, to provide very, very private information.

The President won't move onto the exchanges, will he? No. No, of course he won't. Neither will any of his Cabinet, neither will Kathleen Sibelius, Secretary of HHS. Knowing that, do you understand and can you help the American people understand why we are more concerned, apparently, about the security of our private information? I am speaking now not for myself or my staff. I am speaking for tens of millions of Americans. What would you say to them who are concerned about their security, knowing that they have to do something that the administration and the Cabinet and the Secretary will not have to do? That is, join the exchanges and provide this type of private information.

What could you say to them to make them feel better about that?

Ms. STEMPFLEY. Sir, I have 20 years in the Federal Government, and much of that focused on ensuring that cybersecurity is important to the American public and important to the people who build and operate applications, whether it be in critical infrastructure or in the Federal Government. It has been a passion of mine for a number of years. It is one of the reasons why I am in the job I am in.

Mr. STEWART. Yes. Knowing your background there, and knowing it is your passion and that you have 20 years' of experience, it must be incredibly concerning to you to see some of the failures that—and some of the inherent weaknesses that are apparent within this website. Does that—is that true? Does that bother you, knowing that it is not as secure as it should be?

Ms. STEMPFLEY. I believe the environment that we all operate in today and the dependence on information technology and our critical infrastructure and in other places, it is certainly an area of focus and concern. I am not personally familiar with all of the specifics in health care—in this HHS application. So I am, unfortunately, not in a position to——

Mr. STEWART. Let me ask—let me finish with this last thing. DHS, 99 percent compliant with the FISMA standards, with the Federal Information and Secretary Management Act—99 percent. HHS, 50 percent compliant. Yet HHS did not seek out any council and expertise, any briefings or guidance from DHS in implementing and designing the security around their web page. Any explanation for why they wouldn't seek guidance from DHS, knowing that they were experts on this and that HHS was not?

Ms. STEMPFLEY. As I believe I said—that as we make departments and agencies aware of the capabilities that the Department has it is incumbent upon them to pick the best time in the operational life cycle of their systems and applications for the engagement. I——

Mr. STEWART. Okay. I wish they had done that previous to the portals being open, and not after the fact. But I am out of time, and Mr. Chairman thank you for the hearing.

I yield back.

Chairman McCAUL. I thank the gentleman.

The gentleman from Arizona, Mr. Barber, is recognized.

Mr. BARBER. Thank you, Mr. Chairman. I thank you for having this hearing. Also, thank you to the witnesses for your work as well as for being here today.

I think it has been said, but I certainly agree that the roll-out of the Affordable Care Act has been—the website, in particular, has been just a disaster. I think all of us find it totally unacceptable that we would be in this position. While the ACA offers many benefits to millions of Americans, I have repeatedly said that there are provisions that need to be fixed, there are unintended consequences that need to be dealt with. We need to move on that, I think, in a bipartisan manner in this Congress.

Now we come to a potential new problem. We don't know the magnitude of it because it is early days. Obviously, since so many people have not been able to get on the website we really don't know yet how much personal information might be at risk. Americans are putting data in, in order to even begin the process, that is very sensitive information. I do share the Chairman's concern that the Department of Health & Human Services has a very poor record of cybersecurity, generally speaking. Now, of course, more information than ever before is gonna be available through their system.

I think the American people, generally speaking, are very concerned about their privacy on a number of levels. I mean, we can go into other areas—we won't today—but this is a new area of concern. So having said that, I really believe that unless we can give some assurances that the privacy of information in *HealthCare.gov* is adequately protected it will undermine the American people's confidence in that system and they may choose not even to explore their benefits that are available on that website, when it gets fixed.

So having said that, Mr. Stempfley, your office is responsible for maintaining the security, reliability, and resilience of our Nation's cyber and communications infrastructure. This oversight and general maintenance obviously pertains to our critical infrastructure. But it also pertains to the security of Federal Governments' cyber networks, which interface with the private sector and with individual users to access Federal Government websites.

I would agree—I hope you would agree, we must be vigilant in monitoring and upgrading our systems, and design them to be as ironclad and as impenetrable as possible, particularly those systems that house sensitive user data such as *HealthCare.gov*. Now, having said that, Ms. Stempfley, could you talk, in very specific ways, about the steps that your office has taken to ensure that data that is inputted by American people into the *HealthCare.gov* network, how it has been protected or will be protected, and how have your actions been informed by the attempted incursions that you talked about earlier?

Ms. STEMPFLEY. Sir, the Department of Homeland Security's engagement with the Department of Health & Human Services has been about general threat information provision of best practices and a requirement of compliance reporting. We have provided a verification that Health and Human Services has complied with as domain name security. That is a set of technologies that translate internet addresses, the machine-readable information, to human-readable; so when you type *www.google.com* the internet knows how to translate that.

So we have been able to assure—provide verification that have complied with that level of security in their environment, as well. However, we have not been in a specific architectural conversation with the Department of Health & Human Services on this application.

Mr. BARBER. Have you had any discussions with Health and Human Services subsequent to identifying, as you said, perhaps 16 incursions, actual or attempted?

Ms. STEMPFLEY. We have had an operational conversation between their security operation center and our US–CERT about these particular activities. As I pointed out, these are under investigation. These reports came in in the November 6, 7, and 8 time frame. So there is a period of time where we have to go through a verification and determination.

Mr. BARBER. Yes, I appreciate that you have to check in to make sure that you have some—you can verify what is really going on. But I would urge you, obviously, to speed up that process. Because if and when the website is fully operational—and we are told it will be operational by December—I would expect we will see many more and we need to be prepared for that. I guess my final question is: What plans do you have for on-going monitoring of the security of the website?

Ms. STEMPFLEY. I appreciate the question, sir. A set of capabilities that the Department provides, including one you may know of, is EINSTEIN intrusion detection capabilities, the Center for Medicare and Medicaid Services will be moving its applications behind in the second quarter of calendar year 2013. HHS has been active in attempting to get behind this capability, but had to work through some specific statutory language that was in their statutes. Given that I know this committee has been supportive of, we have been trying to work to get some positive authorization language for these CHS programs that would have shortened that time frame.

Additionally, they have agreed to be an early adopter of the continuous diagnostics and mitigation capability. So we are anxious to get that provided to them. The contract is due to be released today or tomorrow for the acquisition of those capabilities.

Mr. BARBER. Thank you for the extra time, Mr. Chairman.

I yield back.

Chairman McCAUL. Yes, let me thank the gentleman for raising one issue. That is, you know, EINSTEIN has been around for awhile. It seems to me that it should have been applied to this website and to HHS. I think anything we can do to expedite that would certainly be in the best interest of the United States.

So with that, the Chairman now recognizes the gentleman from Montana, Mr. Daines.

Mr. DAINES. Thank you, Mr. Chairman. I spent 20 years in the private sector prior to coming up to Congress. In fact, the last 12 years, an executive with a cloud computing company. Publicly-traded; we took the company public, Oracle acquired us. So the point is, I have worked in the enterprise space with very, very large organizations from around the world and understand the importance, certainly, of privacy as well as reliability.

As a taxpayer, I think it is outrageous as I have seen what has happened here, where we have taken $500 million—by some estimates—to what this project costs—taken out of the pockets of hardworking taxpayers into a system that has failed. The numbers are astounding from the benchmarking. Facebook—Facebook was operational for 6 years and didn't hit the $500 million mark. Twitter, operational for 5 years, $360 million operational investment. Instagram, $57 million investment.

LinkedIn and Spotify didn't even get to the $300 million mark in operational. So there will be a lot of questions, certainly, about the cost and benefits, and value for the taxpayer. That is not why we are here, but I want to pivot over here to the issue of security. CBS News reported Monday evening that Mr. Chao, who was the chief project manager of *HealthCare.gov*, testified last week for 9 hours. CBS is reporting that there was a memo that went out 27 days prior to the launch of the website, on September 3, that said—and this was given to senior officials at CMS—there were two high-risk issues that were redacted for security reasons.

The memo—I see counsel here is giving advice—the memo said the threat and the risk potential is limitless. Sir, I want to make sure she hears the question. The risk and the risk potential, the threat is limitless. It said CMS said the deadlines to fix these were around mid-2014 and early 2015 to address them. In fact, Mr. Chao testified to these security gaps. By the way, when they said "high-risk," what high-risk means is, according to Federal guidelines— "the vulnerability could be expected to have a severe or catastrophic adverse effect on organizational operations, assets, or individuals."

Mr. Chao testified that security gaps, as reported by CBS here, could lead to identity theft, unauthorized access, and misrouted data. As somebody who had to serve large organizations, people would have been fired, the company would have gone under—our company—had we launched a website with these kinds of errors. I understand about risk management and so forth. But it seems that we leaned in to launch—the Federal Government did—knowing that there were high-risk security issues.

Now, as you mentioned in your written testimony, the DHS is the lead for securing and defining Federal civilian unclassified information technology systems and networks against attacks. First, what, if anything, did you recommend as far as policies to CMS and the folks who are running the project here for the *HealthCare.gov*?

Ms. STEMPFLEY. As we engage with chief information officers in the SISOs, we provide a range of information; from general threat briefings, which we provide to the CIO council on a regular basis, to best-practice activities as well as information about FISMA compliance as they go forward. We provide this at a Department level and to participants in the CIO forum and SISO forum. There has not been a specific interaction about—focused on this particular site.

Mr. DAINES. So if, indeed, what CBS reported here and Mr. Chao's testimony last week before a committee—if, indeed, there was limitless potential, as I quote the report, for security risks, knowing this would you have rolled out the *HealthCare.gov* site on October 1, 2013?

Ms. STEMPFLEY. Sir, I am not aware of all of the information that goes into that went into that.

Mr. DAINES. But my question is, if you knew that. As somebody who has the lead here of 20 years' experience, and if I quote your written testimony here, you have the lead for securing and defining Federal and civilian unclassified information, knowing there was limitless potential for security risks, as reported, would you have rolled out, would you have pushed the button to say "go" on October 1, 2013?

Ms. STEMPFLEY. Respectfully, sir, I have been an accrediting official before. These are very difficult decisions that you make as a part of it, and I couldn't speak to a——

Mr. DAINES. But with all due respect, you are the assistant secretary——

Ms. STEMPFLEY. I am——

Mr. DAINES. Leadership is about the buck has to stop somewhere. Would you have made that decision, knowing there were limitless risks, if the report is correct?

Ms. STEMPFLEY. Respectfully, sir, I can't answer a theoretical in this situation. There is a multitude of information that goes into it. The amount of risk that a particular site operates under is certainly one vector or one input point.

Mr. DAINES. All right. Well, I will conclude. The irony, perhaps, in this is that the failure of the website launch on Obamacare may indeed have been the best safeguard for the American people to protect their personal privacy, given the risks now that are being identified in this launch. That is the irony. Because if the American people were prohibited to have, what, six people sign up the first day perhaps that is protecting the American people because they didn't have a chance to enter it in the first place.

Yield back.

Chairman MCCAUL. I thank the gentleman. The gentleman from—Mr. Richmond is recruited, from Louisiana.

Mr. RICHMOND. Mr. Chairman, I guess this hearing is appropriate, and I guess the title is appropriate. It reminds me of the same show, same one-trick pony, that we keep hearing over and over again. The question or concern that I have is that, you know, this is a self-fulfilling prophecy. We keep talking about how bad Obamacare is. We talk about the fact that—discourage everyone that it is not safe. When they don't enroll, some of us will declare victory and take glee in the fact that people don't have health insurance.

At the same time, we run around proclaiming ourselves to be the Christian Right. So I guess my frustration is that there are many things that we could come together and do. We tried last year to come together and pass a cybersecurity bill that was bipartisan. What happened when it was time to mark up that bill and pass it to the floor? The Republican leadership came back and said it went too far, and Republicans had to sit in the room and gut their own cybersecurity bill. Which never made it to the floor, which we never passed.

We sit here today to talk about cybersecurity and how much confidence we should have in *HealthCare.gov*, when we lack confidence in many areas of cybersecurity, which we have done nothing about, we have not passed a bill.

Chairman MCCAUL. Will the gentleman yield?

Mr. RICHMOND. I certainly will.

Chairman MCCAUL. We have conducted over 300 meetings with the private sector. You are referring to last Congress, before I assumed the Chairmanship. I am fully committed to marking up a cybersecurity bill. It is obviously very complex. I want to do it the right way. I appreciate the work that Ms. Stempfley does in terms of cybersecurity. So know that that is just—as the border security passed in a bipartisan way, I am fully committed to doing that work in a bipartisan way.

I yield back.

Mr. RICHMOND. Mr. Chairman, I believe you. I believe that Chairman King wanted to do it also. But it was—and we marked it up in a bipartisan way, and the Republican leadership gutted it. It still didn't make it to the floor. I just say that in the fact that I think that we should all have one purpose. That should be to try to make this a success. Whether you agreed with it or not, it is the law of the land. Let's try to get people health care, get people healthier, and all of those things. Because that is what my interpretation of what we should be doing.

See, and I am not defending the launch. The launch was deplorable. However, what real leadership does is acknowledge that it is deplorable, and fix it. So the question would become when we feel that the website is safer are we going to have another meeting to let the people know that we feel it is safe and encourage them to enroll? I would suggest that the answer would be no because we want to keep that fear out there to reduce the number of people that enroll.

So my question would be, to Ms. Stempfley and to Ms. Correa, basically the title of the committee, which I hope you can give a short answer, but: Just how secure is the information? Do you have faith in the security of the information that people input into the website?

Ms. CORREA. I will give Ms. Stempfley a short break. Thank you for your question. I really couldn't answer that question. Because, as I have indicated from our discussion, what we see is the information that is submitted through the hub to ask for the immigration status of a particular applicant. So I couldn't really talk to the front end of the process. Thank you.

Ms. STEMPFLEY. The America public gives the Government its information in a variety of places and sources. Certainly, in my experience with SISOs, the information security officers throughout the Federal enterprise, they are committed to the obligation that they have in securing these systems and applications. I am not familiar with the specific security features of the 10,000 applications that HHS operates, for example, nor am I familiar with the specific security features of the tens of thousands and hundreds of thousands of applications across the Federal enterprise.

But I do know that in the Department of Homeland Security and with the SISOs that I work on a regular basis they are all—feel passionately about their obligation to protect this information that the America public gives the Government.

Mr. RICHMOND. With the knowledge and expertise that you have in this arena—and you do it every day, and subject-matter expertise—two-part question: Would you enter your information into the exchange, the web portal? If not, would you do it at the end of the month? At what point do you feel it is ready for you to input your information?

Ms. STEMPFLEY. So I, like all of us, put our information in a variety of systems and applications, whether it be my bank, whether it be HHS. I have family information in the HHS system because I am also a taxpayer. I do that, recognizing that whenever I give my information to someone else, under any circumstances, there is a—you know, there is a potential of it being at risk. Whether it be, again, my bank or my electric company or a Federal enterprise. But I do it because I believe the benefit of doing so outweighs whatever that risk might be.

Mr. RICHMOND. Thank you, Mr. Chairman. I yield back.

Chairman MCCAUL. I thank the gentleman.

The Chairman recognizes Mr. Hudson, from North Carolina.

Mr. HUDSON. Thank you, Mr. Chairman. I want to thank you for having this hearing today on this very important topic. You know,

I go home every weekend, I travel my district, I talk to my constituents as much as possible. I have been inundated with calls and mail from my constituents who are deeply concerned about the implementation of the Affordable Care Act. Lately, the news reports about this implementation have focused on the website.

As my colleague said, it has been a disaster. A lot of attention has been focused on the premium increases. North Carolina has been hit harder than most States. Women in our State can expect their rates to triple; men can expect them to quadruple, on average. So a lot of attention has been given to that problem. Then we have heard a lot about loss of coverage. I was talking to a husband in Rockingham the other day whose wife has an acute illness. Their doctors told them that under the Affordable Care Act he is no longer gonna offer them care.

So these are huge problems. But I think what has been lost in all this are these issues, this important issue, of security of our private information. I mean, we have an unprecedented collection of data that the Government is undertaking now of personal information. It is unprecedented that the Government will be collecting these types of information through one process. So it is important that we talk about this and we examine the issues here.

I am disappointed that our—I appreciate your all being here, I appreciate the job you do. It is disappointing, though, that DHS doesn't—isn't able to answer questions about this website. That DHS doesn't have a working understanding of how the security parameters of this website were set up. It is deeply troubling to me that HHS, CMS hasn't asked the folks who are the experts in this—Secretary Stempfley's organization—to help with this implementation.

Why wouldn't you go to the experts when you have got a huge problem? Especially when one of the architects of this website said, "that there is limitless potential for security risks." These are the folks building the website, have said this is a huge problem. Yet they are not asking people who are experts at this how to help them. So I appreciate you being here, Ms. Stempfley, and I am—again, I appreciate the work you do. I am just sorry you weren't more involved in this because the American people deserve every effort we have as a Government to protect them.

So I will focus my questions on a different topic related to this: Ms. Correa, one of our colleagues earlier asked the question what happens if we run a query about someone's citizenship, and we determine that they are here illegally, or an undocumented person. Would you tell me what happens at that point? Is any action taken, any enforcement action on that individual?

Ms. CORREA. Thank you for your question, sir. Again, as I mentioned before, the way the process works is, an individual who presents themselves to a benefit agency, a benefit-granting agency, has to present the information, documentation, on their status. Whether they are a citizenship or they attest, if you will, in their application as to whether or not they are a citizen. If they are not a citizen, then the information is processed as a query.

Mr. HUDSON. If I can interrupt real quick. So it is up to their own word as to whether they are a citizen or not? Self——

Ms. CORREA. They are—when they apply for a benefit, they are filling out a form. On that form they typically attest what their status is, whether——

Mr. HUDSON. So if they choose to mislead and say they are, there is no——

Ms. CORREA. If the agency, the benefit-granting agency, would then, if they attest that they are not a citizen or the Social Security Administration cannot confirm that they are a citizen, would then request their information and process a query through SAVE. SAVE would then go out and ping our databases to identify what the immigration status of that individual is. Typically, our response is either to give what the immigration status is, or if we cannot confirm the immigration status, then we prompt the agency to go through the additional verification steps.

As I described, the second step they could provide additional information, other documentation, or other names that the individual may have used.

Mr. HUDSON. So at the end of the process, if you determine you can't verify they are a citizen, what happens then?

Ms. CORREA. At that point, what we notify the agency to do is to tell this applicant to schedule an appointment with USCIS. We give them the pertinent information to come in and see us. Because there could still be an error in their record. So what we do is try to have an appointment with them, come visit one of our adjudication officers who would then look at their data and look up their information in the records database.

From a SAVE standpoint, we don't take any further action. In other words, we cannot change an individual's record. We do not tamper with the record at all whatsoever. We refer them to one of our adjudications officers, who would then look at the information.

Mr. HUDSON. So as my time is running out—so if someone—you can't verify they are a citizen, they don't come in to see you, that is it. We don't follow up, we don't enforce any immigration law on this illegal person.

Ms. CORREA. Not that I am aware of, sir, but I could confirm that for you.

Mr. HUDSON. If you wouldn't mind, I would appreciate that.

Mr. Chairman, my time has expired. I will yield back.

Chairman MCCAUL. I thank the gentleman.

The gentlelady from Texas, Ms. Jackson Lee, is recognized.

Ms. JACKSON LEE. Mr. Chairman, let me thank you, as well, and Mr. Thompson for this hearing. I always believe that the exercise of our oversight is crucial and important. I think this is the first hearing that I have been in since the loss of Mr. Gerardo Hernandez, and I want to publicly offer my deepest sympathy to him and his family. That is the transportation security officer killed in the line of duty, which reinforces that the U.S. Department of Homeland Security is on the front line, all of your staff and personnel. Would you offer to all of them my deepest sympathy, and to his family.

I wanted to pursue a line of questioning that I think may be helpful to us. First of all, I think it is important to note that this committee invited DHS on November 5, which gives less than 8 days, because of an intervening holiday. So let me thank you for getting your testimony in as quickly as possible. I am not at the agencies, but I do know that there is a layer of review. Although you may be an eloquent writer, you may be a poet laureate, I know that they have to review your work. So I am grateful that you got it in.

One of the things that is happening all over the Congress today, we have got sequester issues, budget issues. But we are dealing with the Affordable Care Act and oversight and homeland security and small business. Certainly, I think it is important to emphasize that the Affordable Care Act is here and it deals with health care. It deals with having the ability to have insurance if you have a pre-existing disease. You can stay on your family's insurance to age 26; preventive care and wellcare examples. It is a solid piece of legislation, and I am grateful that it is here.

Like my colleagues, I am dogged about fixing the technology and, as well, dealing with our privacy and the protection of the privacy of the American people. They should know that. That collectively, as Republicans and Democrats, we will not yield any moment, any minute, any second to protecting their private data. In fact I have joined on to legislation by my colleague, Jim Sensenbrenner, to, in essence, protect American citizens with any reach of privacy beyond what is required for security under the National Security Agency. I take no back seat to that.

So in making that point, I want to just emphasize what I think your work is. Let me go to Ms. Correa, and indicate—and let me just make the point. There is always a representation that Republicans had nothing to do with the Affordable Care Act. Well, it was the Republicans' amendments that required the checking of citizenship and income. That was their language. I am surprised that every time we see a Republican, my friends, they are talking about ending the Affordable Care Act. We never got any amendments in. They got eons of amendments in to this bill.

That was one of them, which requires this simplistic data collection, which is simply that. So I want to ask the question. This is data collection that is basically information on income and citizenship. These fields of data are checked with the records of accuracy. Is that what you do, Mr. Correa? When it comes in, you check the accuracy on citizenship issues?

Ms. CORREA. That is correct.

Ms. JACKSON LEE. All right. Once it is checked, is this information kept or discarded? The inquiry and the information?

Ms. CORREA. We retain the transaction information because we go back and do quality control checks to make sure we are giving accurate information. But we do not download the actual record. Only the immigration status and the——

Ms. JACKSON LEE. So what do you specifically keep?

Ms. CORREA. That information—the immigration status, the——

Ms. JACKSON LEE. When you have an inquiry from HHS.

Ms. CORREA. We retain the inquiry information that was received. The individual's name, their alien registration or I–94 number.

Ms. JACKSON LEE. That you received an inquiry from HHS. How long do you keep it?

Ms. CORREA. I would have to confirm how long.

Ms. JACKSON LEE. Well, you need to get an answer about how long you keep it. Is it protected information?

Ms. CORREA. Yes, it is.

Ms. JACKSON LEE. Have you been hacked?

Ms. CORREA. I am not aware that we have been hacked. I will confirm that for you, but I am not aware that we have been hacked.

Ms. JACKSON LEE. So what is your measure of securing it?

Ms. CORREA. Our system is accredited and certified by our chief information officer.

Ms. JACKSON LEE. Do you do regular checks?

Ms. CORREA. Yes, we do.

Ms. JACKSON LEE. Is it your highest responsibility to protect this information of the American people?

Ms. CORREA. Yes, it is.

Ms. JACKSON LEE. You only get—you get information. Suppose someone is calling for Mr. Garcia, who is a citizen. Are you keeping that inquiry, as well?

Ms. CORREA. In the SAVE program, no. If the individual has attested they are a citizen——

Ms. JACKSON LEE. Yes.

Ms. CORREA [continuing]. And Social Security has been able to confirm, then we would never receive that query.

Ms. JACKSON LEE. All right. So therefore, it is only individuals that may be in question.

Ms. CORREA. Correct.

Ms. JACKSON LEE. You are checking this every day.

Ms. CORREA. Yes, as query——

Ms. JACKSON LEE. Or a regular basis.

Ms. CORREA [continuing]. As queries are received, yes.

Ms. JACKSON LEE. Let me go to Ms. Stempfley. You are the lead agency that coordinates on the cybersecurity for other agencies in the United States. The other—you sort of lead, but you have the point that the other agencies also have responsibility for their cybersecurity. Is that correct?

Ms. STEMPFLEY. Yes, ma'am.

Ms. JACKSON LEE. But as your Department, or your subset Department, DHS, do you feel that there are competencies under your jurisdiction that are attentive to protecting information and preventing hacking through the DHS agency and in coordinating with the other agencies?

Ms. STEMPFLEY. Yes, ma'am, we are very focused on that. My part in the Office of Cybersecurity and Communication, and there are competencies in the data operation centers through the Federal enterprise.

Ms. JACKSON LEE. So what—if we were to keep this system in place, based upon Republican amendments, into the ACA—checking income and immigration status, and that was being held—you deal with cybersecurity, you deal with the potential of hacking or information going in a different direction that it should not go. What is your level of confidence and your level of competence that you are working in a coordinated fashion, but have the level of technology that can assure, as much as possible, the protection of this information?

Ms. STEMPFLEY. So I am very grateful both for the question and for this committee's continued support of DHS authorities and support of important programs that will improve both the competence and confidence in this area. As we have been talking about the continuous diagnostic and mitigation activity and the FISMA reform efforts that will both increase the awareness across the Federal enterprise of the operational risks that systems are operating under on a daily basis, and enable accrediting officials to take that into account in something more often than annual or every 3-year accreditation processes. As well as I believe I——

Ms. JACKSON LEE. But are you confident in your present structure in your oversight on cybersecurity? That is, information is being gathered; you don't compare this to the Veterans Administration loss of 24 million records under the Bush administration. We are not at that——

Ms. STEMPFLEY. We are not at that——

Ms. JACKSON LEE. We are not at that point. So are you confident, as this huge process is going forward, that we have a system in place to protect that information?

Ms. STEMPFLEY. Yes, ma'am.

Ms. JACKSON LEE. I thank you very much for your answers.

Mr. Chairman, I hope that we can rid ourselves of sequestration so we can invest more in the work that is being done by Ms. Stempfley and Ms. Correa. I yield back, thank you.

Chairman MCCAUL. I thank the gentlelady. Also, the gentlelady is correct that we did put provisions in to assure that only those legally in the country received this—that were eligible under this law. Also, we both agreed that if you have a preexisting condition you cannot be denied coverage, as well.

I will just add lastly that we did make a request for the statement, the opening statements, on August 31, and that is almost 2 weeks. I am sorry, October 31, nearly 2 weeks.

So with that, the Chairman now recognizes the gentleman from Pennsylvania, Mr. Barletta.

Ms. JACKSON LEE. Well, Mr. Chairman, I thank you. We recognize the pounding of work on these various hard-working public servants. As you well know, we were in the middle of a Government shutdown, and so I appreciate timely responses, Mr. Chairman. I hope that they will work to get timely responses.

I yield back, Mr. Chairman. Thank you.

Chairman MCCAUL. Yes, right. The Chairman recognizes Mr. Barletta.

Mr. BARLETTA. Thank you, Mr. Chairman. Ms. Stempfley, I would like to continue on and follow up on some questions that Mr. Meehan had brought up earlier. Secretary Sibelius admitted that convicted felons could be hired as exchange navigators because there was no background checks system in place for these individuals. Why aren't we conducting background checks?

Ms. STEMPFLEY. Respectfully, sir, my area of expertise is cybersecurity. Physical security and personal security are outside of that area. I am happy to take the question, but I could only speculate and that seems inappropriate.

Mr. BARLETTA. Okay. With your expertise in cybersecurity, do you think it would be a good idea to do background checks on these navigators?

Ms. STEMPFLEY. I believe one of the things that we certainly focus on is assuring the protection against——

Mr. BARLETTA. I am just asking: Do you think it would be a good idea to do background checks on the navigators?

Ms. STEMPFLEY. I am happy—again, sir, I would be——

Mr. BARLETTA. No. Do you think it would be a good idea? That is all I am asking, real simple. Do you think it would be a good idea to do background checks on navigators?

Ms. STEMPFLEY. I believe that all individuals should be vetted——

Mr. BARLETTA. Good idea, bad idea?

Ms. STEMPFLEY [continuing]. Prior to access to the information that they provided.

Mr. BARLETTA. Good idea, bad idea?

Ms. STEMPFLEY. I am not trying to evade, sir. I believe that all individuals should be vetted prior to access.

Mr. BARLETTA. I am not gonna get an answer. Ms. Correa, my time—I was mayor for quite some time. I remember one individual. He was in the country illegally. It took our detectives 5 hours to determine who he was. He had five Social Security cards, five different identities. You suggested a little earlier that illegal immigrants won't try to go through the system, and because you are using the SAVE system. I am gonna disagree with you.

That is simply not true. We know, for a fact—is the SAVE system used for the SNAP program, do you know?

Ms. CORREA. Not that I am aware of. Sir, may I clarify? I wasn't trying to imply that an illegal alien wouldn't try. What I was trying to make clear was that they would have to have some form of documentation——

Mr. BARLETTA. Do you think that they can get through the system?

Ms. CORREA. It is hard to say. It would depend on the documentation that they present.

Mr. BARLETTA. Well, we know for a fact that illegal immigrants are able to access many Federal benefits through fraudulent documentations. We know that for a fact. That is—you know, so I don't believe this Government program will really be any different. There is nothing that indicates that it will. So if you determine an applicant is in the country illegally, am I correct, there is no enforcement action taken?

Ms. CORREA. The SAVE program isn't making a determination whether that individual is here illegally, or not. What the SAVE program is doing is based on the information that was presented to us. We are going out and checking the Federal——

Mr. BARLETTA. Well, it does tell if they are a lawful citizen.

Ms. CORREA. Whether they are here as——

Mr. BARLETTA. Right. So, you determine that this individual is not lawfully here, there is no enforcement action taken?

Ms. CORREA. As I explained earlier, the determination that we make is whether we can confirm that individual's immigration status and provide that information——

Mr. BARLETTA. Okay, so you determine that individual's status, that that person is not legally present in the United States. Is there any enforcement action taken?

Ms. CORREA. We don't determine whether the person is here legally or not because we are not seeing the individual. All we are seeing is the information that comes through the query.

Mr. BARLETTA. So if the information that is presented is fraudulent, what happens?

Ms. CORREA. We don't have a way of determining if that information is fraudulent.

Mr. BARLETTA. So we don't know.

Ms. CORREA. As it is presented.

Mr. BARLETTA. So it doesn't seem like there is really any guard for illegal immigrants to access this program as they have been able to access many Government programs. We know there is fraud in so many Government programs. How can we assure the American people that this time we got it? This time we are not gonna let people illegally get into a program that they are not rightfully entitled to.

Ms. CORREA. Sir, if I may explain. I appreciate your question. The benefit-granting agency is the organization that is receiving the information from the individual and is privy to that information. They submit a query to us, where we go back and confirm——

Mr. BARLETTA. But if the information is fraudulent.

Ms. CORREA. What we do is, the only way we could ever determine that is if somebody actually sees the documents and compares them to the individuals. That is why if we cannot confirm immigration status we do ask them to set up an—to refer the individual——

Mr. BARLETTA. I am not real confident that we are gonna be able to stop it. I just want to close, Mr. Chairman. I am a huge baseball fan, huge baseball fan. Now that the Affordable Care Act has been rolled out, we find that the website doesn't work, that Americans' personal information is at risk, that felons could be navigators. This is only the first inning. The Obamacare batting average is not so good.

If the Affordable Care Act was a baseball player, and I was the manager, I would bench him. Thank you.

Chairman MCCAUL. I thank the gentleman for his analogy.

With that, I want to thank the members of the first panel for their valuable testimony here today. With that, this panel is dismissed, and the clerk will prepare for the witness table for a second panel.

I am pleased to welcome the second panel to today's hearing. Mr. Luke Chung is the president at FMS, Incorporated, a company he founded in 1986. In addition to being a primary author and designer of many FMS commercial products, Mr. Chung has personally provided consulting services to a wide range of clients. A recognized database expert, highly-regarded authority in the Microsoft Access developer community, Mr. Chung was featured by Microsoft as an Access hero during Access' 10-year anniversary celebration. Mr. Chung, really good to have you here.

Our second witness, Mr. Waylon Krush is the chief executive officer of Lunar, Incorporated. He served over 15 years of experience in critical infrastructure protection, information operation, signal intelligence, system and telecommunications exploitation, and certification and accreditation. Prior to becoming CEO, Mr. Krush was a senior InfoSec engineer in AT&T's advanced systems division and chief of the information assurance group with the GRC/TSC.

The witnesses' full written statements will appear in the record. I now recognize Mr. Chung for 5 minutes for his opening statement.

STATEMENT OF LUKE CHUNG, PRESIDENT, FMS, INC.

Mr. CHUNG. Well, thank you very much for having me. I am the president and founder of FMS, Inc., a privately-held software development firm located in Vienna, Virginia. For 27 years, we have offered commercial software products and services. We have tens of thousands of customers in over 100 countries, including 90 of the Fortune 100. In response to 9/11, we created a product, Sentinel Visualizer, a link analysis solution for the counterterrorism, defense, and law enforcement communities.

That work led to our only outside investor, InQTel, the CIA's venture capital arm. We also have a professional solutions group that creates custom software. An example is a humanitarian relief logistics system we built for the Pan-American Health Organization and United Nations. It is deployed around the world, and I presume it is in heavy use right now in the Philippines. I am a graduate of Harvard College, with a bachelor's degree in engineering and a masters in physical oceanography.

On October 1, I visited the *HealthCare.gov* website, eager to see what it offered. As a small business owner, I am faced with the challenge of purchasing health insurance for my company and family. Unfortunately, my shopping experience failed due to technical problems with the website. It was not designed to be customer-friendly, appeared to be developed by amateurs, and seemed to be untested. I sensed the site would not work for one person, much less a National enterprise quality solution that was needed.

I wrote a blog post that day providing a nonpartisan technical assessment entitled *"HealthCare.gov* is a Technical Disaster." I warned that the problems were far deeper than too many users, and concluded this would be a huge public relations problem that could doom the Affordable Care Act. That is what I saw on Day 1. My blog post went viral. After a week, I was quoted in the *New York Times* and have been on many radio and National TV news shows, which led to my appearance before you today.

I would like to say that my firm is not involved with the development of *HealthCare.gov*, we did not bid on any portion of the project, and I am here to provide my perspective as a small business owner, someone experienced with database web development and familiar with the Government contracting process. Since I don't like being a critic without offering solutions, on October 14 I wrote another blog post outlining how *HealthCare.gov* could be built properly; a site that would match the customer buying process, be quicker to develop, easier to test, be more robust, support more users, and be more secure.

It is not that complicated. This website does not provide health care. It does not even provide health insurance. It is supposed to let consumers shop and choose among health insurance plans, and then apply for a subsidy. It is essentially the automation of a paper form. So how did we get here? Originally, I thought the design decisions of *HealthCare.gov* were created by amateurs who didn't know what they were doing. Now I see the design decisions can be explained by considering what the contractors would choose to maximize profitability at every step of the way.

The current Government contracting system discourages technically-qualified companies like mine. The big Government contractors are great at winning contracts, protesting lost awards, and generating change orders. They are not known for their technical expertise and would unlikely survive in the private sector. This is a complete breakdown in managing technology investments. Policymakers and politicians do not understand if a project should cost a million dollars or $200 million, or the decisions they make that impact price.

For instance, $200 million, at a generous $200 per-hours, is 1 million man-hours. That is 500 man-years. Forget the money. What could these contractors have possibly been doing with all that time? I propose that the Government needs to create a nonpartisan technology accountability office, TAO, similar to the GAO that is capable of assessing and managing Government technology projects. The TAO also needs to be empowered to enforce accountability.

Bad performance does not seem to prevent contractors from winning new contracts. Multi-year and permanent bans should target underperforming vendors and their owners and the managers. Get refunds. In the private sector, vendors that fail like this would rarely be allowed back in an organization. In conclusion, I have provided written testimony with additional examples, information, and recommendations on investigating how so much money was spent for so little. This is a scandal beyond *HealthCare.gov*.

Unfortunately, the Federal Government has paid for even larger software projects that were never deployed. Without changing the processes, there will be more technology disasters in our future. Just so you know, while I was able to complete my *HealthCare.gov* application on October 1, it remains in progress as of last night. Thank you for inviting me. I look forward to your questions.

[The prepared statement of Mr. Chung follows:]

PREPARED STATEMENT OF LUKE CHUNG

NOVEMBER 13, 2013

SUMMARY

About Me and FMS, Inc.

I'm the president and founder of FMS, Inc., a privately-held software development firm in Vienna, Virginia. For 27 years, we've created database solutions with a combination of commercial products and services. In response to 9/11, our Advanced Systems Group created Sentinel Visualizer, a product for the counter-terrorism, defense, and law enforcement communities that led to our only outside investor, InQTel, the CIA's venture capital arm. We have tens of thousands of customers in over 100 countries, including 90 of the Fortune 100. Our Professional Solutions Group has created a wide range of custom solutions, some which are more complex than *Healthcare.gov*, but never more expensive. I'm a graduate of Harvard College with a bachelor's in engineering and a master's in physical oceanography.

My Experience with Healthcare.gov

On October 1, I visited *Healthcare.gov* to get an insurance quote for my family. The experience was so terrible that I documented the technical problems I encountered and wrote a blog post about it. I could tell immediately from the nature of the crashed I encountered that the site was not ready by prime time. It had a terrible design that was not consumer-friendly, seemed to be coded by amateurs, and wasn't tested. I could tell the site would not work for one person much less the expected load.

The blog post I wrote on October 1 went viral as people began to understand the problems were deeper than too many users. That led to being quoted in the *New York Times* and appearing on radio and news shows such as CBS, CNN, Fox, MSNBC, NBC, Hannity, Greta, Al Jazeera, Geraldo, etc. Throughout the period, I've learned more about the website and its many problems both political and technical.

Healthcare.gov Overview

This website should not be that difficult to build. It doesn't provide health care. It doesn't even provide health insurance. It's comparing plans and applying for a subsidy. It's the automation of a paper form.

Security Implications

Security is considered at the beginning of a project, not at the end. Avoiding the collection of unnecessary personal information is the first step to reducing security issues. Separating the user experience from back-end legacy systems is another. The pressure to make a software solution "work" is not conducive to good security. There are ways to improve the user experience, scalability, and security.

Contractor Abuse of Taxpayers

Healthcare.gov is just one example of a software project gone awry that Government contractors profited at the expense of taxpayers. I originally thought the website was created by people who didn't know what they were doing; that they were trying to do too much in an unnecessarily complicated and thorough manner. My thoughts have evolved and I now feel that it's designed quite cleverly to maximize taxpayer expense. This is a scandal that needs to be investigated. Follow the money and I believe you'll see design decisions that led to increased costs. There are ways to improve governance to fix this.

BACKGROUND

Thank you for inviting me to your hearing.

About FMS, Inc.

I'm Luke Chung; the president and founder of FMS, Inc., a privately-held software development firm located in Vienna, Virginia. Since 1986, FMS has provided software products and development services to commercial and Government agencies. Over 27 years, we've created a wide range of database solutions helping organizations make better decisions based on data. These important decisions include delivering services, managing operations, understanding finances, increasing accuracy, improving customer service, making fewer errors, targeting criminals, making more money, and increasing efficiency. We have tens of thousands of customers in over 100 countries.

In the 1990s, we became the world's leading provider of commercial products for Microsoft Access with 12 solutions to help people better analyze data, automate e-mail blasts, create better solutions, eliminate errors, and provide system administration.

In response to 9/11, we created the FMS Advanced Systems Group to use link analysis and social network analysis (SNA) to find hidden relationships among people, places, and events. That led to the creation of our Sentinel Visualizer product that helps analysts in the counter-terrorism, defense, and law enforcement communities, both in the United States and abroad. Sentinel Visualizer led to our only outside investor, InQTel, the CIA's venture capital arm.

In addition to our commercial off-the-shelf products, the FMS Professional Solutions Group has created custom database applications for a wide range of customers. Examples include the Logistics Support System for the Pan American Health Organization sponsored by six U.N. agencies. It coordinates humanitarian relief logistics for disaster zones and is deployed with language localization features in over 100 countries, including the Philippines. FMS also created a course management system for the Defense Acquisition University, which provides non-military training to all branches of the DoD. FMS has also created custom solutions for event management, e-commerce, logistics, education, health care, public works, nonprofits, and businesses.

About Me

I'm originally from New York, grew up in Orlando and Sarasota, Florida, and am a graduate of Harvard College. I have a bachelor's degree in engineering, and a master's degree in Physical Oceanography. Prior to founding FMS, I worked as a management consultant at Strategic Planning Associates/Mercer.

- Current member and past president of the Washington, DC Chapter of the Entrepreneurs Organization.
- Serve on the Business and Community Advisory Council to the Fairfax County Virginia Public School Superintendent.
- Serve on the Information Technology Policy Advisory Committee to assist the Fairfax County Board of Supervisors oversee county technology investments. The committee exists because the supervisors recognized years ago they were unable to provide the proper governance over their technology investments.

Caveats

My testimony is based on my personal experiences and opinions. I am an observer to the *Healthcare.gov* website and am not personally involved with its design and development. Any suggestions of incompetence or wrongdoing are comments intended for further investigation by the committee.

My Perspective

I am providing my testimony from a non-partisan perspective focused on my decades of experience creating database solutions, the challenges of running a small business, and having observed how the Government contracting world works.

In 27 years running FMS, I've experienced multiple Government administrations, economic cycles, and changes with technology. I run a small business and have responsibilities to my clients, firm, employees, and family. These obligations include buying health insurance.

EXPERIENCE WITH HEALTHCARE.GOV ON OCTOBER 1

On October 1, I visited the *Healthcare.gov* website to get an insurance quote for my family. I wanted to see what policies were available and how they compared in features and price to what my small business is currently purchasing in our group plan.

What started as a simple shopping experience turned into a venture inside the technically worst website I've ever visited. It was so bad that I started documenting the bugs I encountered. I was shocked because the mistakes were so amateurish that it seemed the website was created by people who had never been paid to write commercial software. Based on my experience, I realized that if those types of bugs existed, the website had huge problems way beyond the number of users. I sensed that it would not support one user, much less the millions expected.

The shocking part is that this website should be very simple:

- It does not provide health care;
- It does not even provide health insurance;
- It's supposed to let consumers compare and choose among insurance plans;
- It's supposed to generate a subsidy, if any, to buy insurance;
- It is essentially the automation of a 12-page paper form.

I shared my findings in a company blog post entitled *Healthcare.gov is a Technological Disaster* (*http://blog.fmsinc.com/healthcare-gov-is-a-technological-disaster/*)—See Appendix A. It includes screenshots of the crashes and suggested that I was embarrassed for my profession for delivering such junk. It looked like the developers never used or tested it. I concluded that the quality of the work wouldn't pass a computer science class and that there would be huge Public Relations problems that could doom the entire Affordable Care Act. That's what I saw on Day 1.

Response to My Blog Post

While the contractors and administration tried to spin the problems as the result of too many users, my blog post—which provided a non-partisan, technical evaluation of *Healthcare.gov*—started getting picked up by multiple websites. And through the power of social media, it went viral.

Within a week, I was quoted in a *New York Times* article which was followed by interviews with radio and National TV news channels including CBS, CNN, Fox, MSNBC, NBC, Sean Hannity, Al Jazeera, Greta van Susteren, Geraldo Rivera, etc. It has led to this testimony.

Offering Solutions

Since I don't like being a critic without offering possible solutions, on October 14, I wrote another blog post outlining how *Healthcare.gov* can be properly built: *Creating a Healthcare.gov Web Site that Works (http://blog.fmsinc.com/creating-a-healthcare-gov-web-site-that-works/)* see Appendix B.

My suggestions would a website that would better address the needs of the customer, be simpler to develop, easier to test, more robust, support more simultaneous users, and be more secure. It would separate the shopping experience and an estimate of a subsidy from the actual application to receive a subsidy (the part that needs to be secure). The marketplace would be the central site where it would be easy to compare insurance plans before worrying about pricing and subsidies. The site would be hosted on commercial cloud providers that could scale to support huge numbers of simultaneous users. It would use commercial business software that would significantly reduce the amount of code that needs to be written and tested, which would also reduce the security risk.

Healthcare.gov Observations

Here are my observations about the technical issues I encountered on the *Healthcare.gov* website:
- It's poorly designed. It doesn't address the needs of a consumer trying to shop for something, nor is it designed to support lots of users or high security.
- It's poorly developed. The site has such amateurish errors that it appears to be created by inexperienced developers.
- It's not tested, or if it was tested, the test plan was woefully inadequate.
- In my experience, encountering that many bugs in such a short period of time indicates that was only the tip of the iceberg with many more bugs below the surface. As bugs are fixed, more bugs will be found since those sections were never adequately tested before.
- The management team and contractors seemed to think the site was production quality on October 1. It clearly wasn't, which would indicate that those people don't understand what production quality means. They shouldn't be involved with the project since we've experienced what they consider shipping quality. I do not consider what was delivered to be beta (test) quality.

SECURITY IMPLICATIONS

Lack of competent technical oversight not only leads to waste, but to potentially devastating security vulnerabilities if complex systems that millions of people depend on are undermined or brought to their knees by attackers. Technology alone cannot deliver security, and the more complex a system is, the harder it is to secure against known threats, much less unknown ones which are sure to emerge in the future. When developers operate under deadline pressure, they tend to cut corners to "just get it to work", generating fresh security vulnerabilities and bugs.
- Nothing is ever perfectly secure.
- Security has to be considered at the beginning of the project, not at the end.
- The most important part of security is to NOT collect secure information unnecessarily.
- The next step is to minimize the places where security is necessary. The sections in which users shop for insurance policies, get an estimate of the subsidy, and buy a policy without a subsidy should not require any security.
- Another design consideration is to create as few places of vulnerability as possible. That means fewer screens, fewer places where data changes hands, and running secure processes off-line separate from the user interface.
- The skills to build a secure web database application are far more advanced than the skills the existing developers failed to exhibit. A chain is only as strong as its weakest link.

CONTRACTOR INCENTIVES

Originally, I thought the design decisions of the *Healthcare.gov* site were done by amateurs who didn't know what they were doing. I'm now moving away from that conclusion.

Instead, I'm seeing how the design decisions may have been made to maximize taxpayer expense and vendor profitability.

Government Contractors

The current Government contracting system excludes technically-qualified companies by making it difficult for them to bid and work on Government projects. The companies that specialize in Government contracts are good at winning Government contracts, protesting lost awards, and creating change orders. They are not known for their technical expertise. Their strategies and operations would not be competitive in the private sector.

Currently there is no downside for failure to deliver on a Government contract. There is nothing to prevent failed vendors from bidding on future projects or being suspended from existing projects.

Abusing Taxpayers

I don't know how the decisions were made, but if I look at it from the contractors' perspective with the knowledge that the budget was essentially unlimited, it would explain how choices were made to add complexity, increase billable hours, purchase more hardware and bandwidth, and maximize profits.

Of course, the big mistake was not delivering a quality solution. Unlike many other IT projects that have failed in the Federal Government, this one let the public experience the quality of the deliverables.

Examples of areas that maximize profits:
- Performing an identity check for each visitor. Is the credit agency paid for each check?
- Creating a user login in three screens rather than one? Was the contractor paid per screen? Was there consideration that more screens use more resources? Why ask for secret questions?
- The email confirmation process requires almost immediate confirmation. My 30-minute delay in responding canceled my account and required creating a new login. Why does this feature exist?
- Why are the screens to fill out the application one question per screen? Why not put all the questions on one screen to minimize the complexity, data exchanges, and improve scalability and security? Were contractors paid based on the number of questions and screens?
- Why ask optional questions such as race that are not part of the subsidy process?

Addressing Contractor Complaints

From what I can see, the contractors are trying their best to deflect blame:
- There are claims the Government was changing the design at the last minute and there wasn't enough time for testing. On every project I've worked on, designs are always changing and there has never been too much time for testing. It's the responsibility of the contractor to provide the guidance and services to ensure success.
- There are claims that individual portions were working but the overall system was not. Based on what I observed, the website wasn't working even if the overall system wasn't tested. My belief is that both the individual portions AND the integrated system were not working.

Where Did the Money Go?

I don't understand how the contractors could have charged the taxpayers so much money. At $200 million at a generous $200 per hour, that's 1,000,000 man hours. That's 500 man-years. Now the numbers are even larger. Where did all that time go?

TECHNOLOGY MANAGEMENT RECOMMENDATIONS

This is a complete breakdown in managing technology investments. People do not understand when a project should cost $1 million vs. $100 million. In the private sector, a $1 million budget to build a website is huge. The Government needs to remember that buying from companies that specialize in Government contracting is not the same as vendors who are competitive in the private sector.

Create a Technology Assessment Office

A Technology Assessment Office (TAO), a non-partisan entity similar to the GAO that is capable of assessing and managing Government technology projects. Policy makers, politicians, and bureaucrats do not possess the technology skills to keep up with the rapidly-changing technology options. They also don't understand what technology should cost or the implications their decisions have on cost, security, and other options. My serving on the Fairfax County Technology Policy Advisory Committee is an example of this type of governance.

Enforce Accountability

Past performance is considered an important part of winning Government contracts but it doesn't seem to prevent contractors involved with failed projects to continue winning new contracts. If qualifications matter for selecting contractors, when do contractors ever get permanently banned? Multi-year or permanent bans should target underperforming vendors to prevent them from bidding on new contracts and removed from existing ones.

In the private sector, vendors that fail would rarely be allowed back. Do we have a too-big-to-exclude policy?

An exhaustive investigation and audit of the *Healthcare.gov* project would help determine the various points of systemic failure in order to ensure that a debacle of this magnitude never happens again.

Experience of the Development Team

The experience of the vendor is important, but what's most important is the experience of the people actually doing the work. Given my sense that the developers were quite junior, it would be interesting to learn their previous experience building commercial database websites, what they were being paid, and what the taxpayers were charged. Make sure people involved with the entire life of the project are questioned, and not just the ones remaining today.

Development Management and Environment

- How were the deliverables designed, scheduled, and delivered?
- How were the teams managed?
- What code reviews were held, and by whom?
- What development, testing, and staging environments were employed?
- Was there a test plan? If so, what were the results of the test plan before October 1? What bugs were considered acceptable for deployment?
- How did the test plan change and who was paid for the October 1 that was so bad?
- Is load testing and balancing in place?
- What kind of security reviews, threat analyses, and mitigation strategies were undertaken?
- What kinds of security vulnerabilities were detected, and when are they scheduled to be addressed? How are security issues addressed on an on-going basis?

Technology Selections

- Why did they take such a strong stand on using open-source "free" software rather than commercial business software that would require less customization (and therefore cost less with fewer security vulnerabilities)? (*TheAtlantic.com*, June 28, 2013, *Healthcare.gov: Code Developed by the People and for the People, Released Back to the People*)
- Why did they create their own cloud rather than using better and cheaper commercial cloud providers? Especially when large portions of this site do not need any security.

Design Flaws and Bugs

Secretary Sebelius and HHS have announced that they've fixed hundreds of bugs, which indicates that there are likely hundreds more yet to be found. No matter how many bugs are fixed, the unintended consequence is that more will inevitably crop up elsewhere in the code base. Is the current website being redesigned to make it work properly for consumers, or are they instead trying to make the existing flawed design functional? Poorly-designed systems are nearly impossible to rescue, and inevitably lead to further support costs down the road. When a complex system is created by multiple vendors with no technical managerial oversight, it is inevitable that systemic flaws will lead only to finger-pointing and recrimination, not to solid, functioning software.

Number of Concurrent Users

The heaviest demand day was not October 1, but will be the day of the deadline to sign up. It's the equivalent of April 15 for the IRS. How are they preparing for that? How many simultaneous users can they support, and what happens if the number of users exceeds that? Is load balancing in place? Are we buying lots of equipment for that one day that will sit idle afterwards? Totally unnecessary if a commercial cloud provider is used.

There are policy implications if the system crashes and people are shut out before the deadline.

What Are They Thinking?

- How could they have possibly thought the site was ready to go on October 1? There was a seminar scheduled on *HowTo.gov* to showcase how the contractors created this great website but it was postponed due to the Government shut-down and later canceled.

- Are they redesigning the website to make it work properly for consumers or are they trying to make the existing bad design work?

A More Open Policy

- Many companies could have created the *Healthcare.gov* website or similar data-base websites. Why is it so difficult for technically-qualified companies to bid and work on Government projects?
- Why isn't the data on the insurance policies, pricing, and formulas for subsidies opened in a manner that the private sector can create their own website mar-ketplaces?

CONCLUSIONS

Overall, I'm embarrassed as an American to watch my President and Cabinet Sec-retary talk about website design, development, and testing, and promoting 800 num-bers. They should be focused on policy and things like Iran and North Korea. Websites should be taken care of at a much lower level and certainly no higher than the CTO.

The underlying problem of *Healthcare.gov* lies in the way that Government con-tracts are awarded. Our way of life is becoming more, not less, dependent on tech-nology every day, yet there is no one at the highest levels of Government capable of determining when the Government is being ripped off.

Taxpayers made a significant investment with the contractors to expect a func-tional *Healthcare.gov* website. While there may be some excuse for complexity with connecting to legacy databases in various agencies, I don't see any reasonable ex-cuse why the user experience would be so defective or the costs so high.

This is a scandal beyond *Healthcare.gov* and touches on the entire way the Gov-ernment purchases software solutions. Unfortunately, the Federal Government has paid for even larger software projects that were never functional.

The need for a bi-partisan Technology Accountability Office to investigate and reg-ulate technology at the Federal level is urgent and immediate; not only to stem the hemorrhage of taxpayer dollars, but to ensure the security and viability of the es-sential systems millions of Americans depend on.

Taxpayers paid Super Bowl ticket prices and were delivered a high school football game. Follow the money.

ATTACHMENTS

APPENDIX 1.—BLOG POST: HEALTHCARE.GOV IS A TECHNOLOGICAL DISASTER

This was the blog post I wrote on October 1 providing a non-partisan technical review of the *Healthcare.gov* website.

Finally Here

October 1, the Affordable Care Act (Obamacare) website *Healthcare.gov* finally went live today.

I was eager to personally review what was being offered and cut through the hoopla and criticism. I had previously written *FMS Receives Health Insurance Pre-mium Refund from the Affordable Care Act,* so my expectations were high.

From the previously published rates for Virginia, the cost of insurance premiums for individuals and families was considerably lower than what FMS currently pays for our group plan. Business plans aren't available yet, but the individual plans should be a good indicator. I wasn't interested in the subsidies; I simply wanted to know the prices for the different plan options.

Applying for Coverage

So I went on-line to *Healthcare.gov* around 5:30 A.M. to apply for my family and see what it would cost. As expected, you create a log-in with email confirmation, and fill out a Wizard to select the options. It's similar to many other instances I've applied on-line for credit cards and other forms of insurance. How tough could it be? Technically, it's a very simple data entry application that should generate a quote at the end.

What a Mess!

Unfortunately, what should be a simple process is a complete software technology disaster. The logical flow of the application to register, log-in, and fill out the data for a family was horrendously inefficient. It seemed like the person who designed it, had never used it. Or maybe didn't have a family which required filling out the same information for each member of the family.

Just the initial process of creating a log-in required multiple secret questions and other unnecessary data for getting a quote. Sure that may be necessary for the final acceptance, but it's a complete waste of time and web resources initially. The system should expedite the process as much as possible to get people a quote without subsidies, then ask for more information to calculate the subsidies if desired. Since I later discovered it never generates a quote, it may not really matter anyway. What were the designers thinking?

Overly Complex Data Entry

As for my family, I not only had to identify my spouse, my two kids, their relationship to me, but also their relationship to my wife, and even their relationship to each other! What? Given the prior information, obvious defaults could be offered. The selection of race was also more complicated than it should be. Here's an idea that may not have occurred to the designers: Maybe the kids should default to inherit their parents' races. That's how inheritance works. And does race impact pricing? If not, why ask?

The system crashed several times for me and had problems when I logged back in. It seemed like the system wasn't even tested. Here are some screenshots:

Screenshot 1: Gibberish

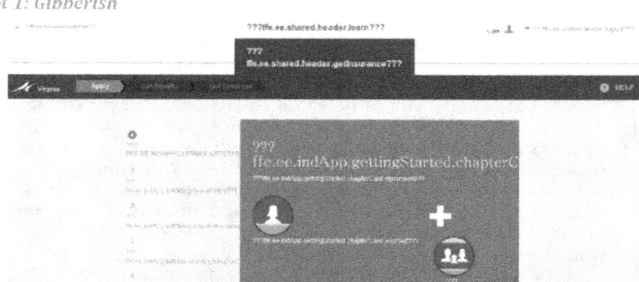

What the hell is that? How could that get through testing much less production?

Screenshot 2: Error form with no data

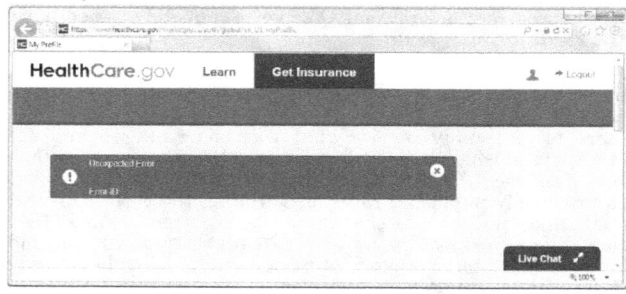

Having error handling to catch unexpected crashes is a Best Practice in application development. It should tell the user what went wrong, what to do next, and gracefully exit the system. This page does none of that. The error message and error number are blank. Who knows what went wrong? Useless and amateurish. They do have a Live Chat button. I wonder what I would chat with them about with this crash.

Screenshot 3: Cascading errors

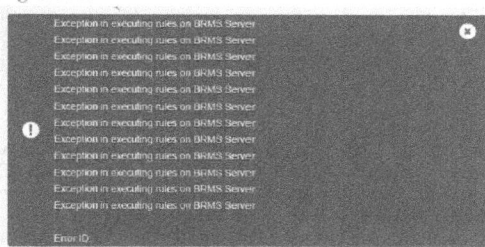

In this screenshot a series of errors appear to be triggered without meaningful explanation. Embarrassing.

Logging Back in and Repeating

If anything, I'm persistent. I not only had my original goal to see the premium prices, I was now intrigued to discover how poorly designed, developed, and tested this application was. Eventually, I was able to finish. Took about an hour.

However, rather than receiving a quote immediately, it's now being "processed". For what? It shouldn't be held up for pre-existing conditions which ACA eliminates. I would expect it to be some mathematical, logical formula that would generate the results. I presume it's because that part of the application isn't built yet. Although my application is submitted, given the crashes, I'm not sure what data it has. We'll see.

Authors of Healthcare.gov

A few months ago, I read this article about how the site was being built and was impressed: *Healthcare.gov: Code Developed by the People and for the People, Released Back to the People.*

In hindsight, it appears the authors have a philosophical bias toward Open Source and "people power." That's all fine and dandy if it works, but this site doesn't. To deliver such low quality results requires multiple process breakdowns. It just proves you can create bad solutions independent of the choice of technology.

Technical Software Conclusions

What should clearly be an enterprise-quality, highly-scalable software application, felt like it wouldn't pass a basic code review. It appears the people who built the site don't know what they're doing, never used it, and didn't test it.

I actually experienced many more problems than the screenshots I captured. Had I known I was performing a Quality Assurance assignment, I would have kept better documentation of typos, unclear directions, bad grammar, poorly-designed screens, and other crashes. My bad!

It makes me wonder if this is the first paid application created by these developers. How much did the contractor receive for creating this awful solution? Was it awarded to the lowest price bidder? As a taxpayer, I hope we didn't pay a premium for this because it needs to be rebuilt. And fixing, testing, and redeploying a live application like this is non-trivial. The managers who approved this system before it went live should be held accountable, along with the people who selected them.

FMS PROFESSIONAL SERVICES GROUP

Our Professional Solutions Group has created many mission-critical, custom software applications where scalability, reliability, and quality are paramount. For instance, we built the Logistics Support System for International Humanitarian Relief for the United Nations where lives are dependent on accurate, timely data on a global scale.

SENTINEL VISUALIZER

We've also created a database link analysis program for the intelligence and law enforcement communities.

I know what's involved in creating great software, and this ain't it. *Healthcare.gov* is simply an insurance quote system. As a software developer, I'm embarrassed for my profession. If FMS ever delivered such crap, I'd be personally inconsolable. This couldn't pass an introductory computer science class.

Overall Conclusions

This is going to be a huge public relations mess that could doom the whole initiative. Maybe they can blame the problems on too many users even if that weren't the real cause, but it's not going to be fixed with a few weekend tweaks and throwing more hardware at this. The application process asks too many unnecessary questions and repeatedly crashes. Since 9 A.M. and as of this evening, the site no longer lets you apply. I presume it got overloaded or someone finally discovered how broken it is and pulled the plug. Given what I experienced, it needs to be off-line until it's corrected. Meanwhile, I'd be highly concerned about the security of the data people enter given all the crashes I encountered.

Of course, software problems with the application process are not the reason to abandon health care reform. As a small business owner, we face the highest premiums for the lowest coverage. I applaud the efforts to reform health insurance and look forward to working in a constructive, rather than destructive, manner to improve this. I presume once these issues are resolved, I'll have more options for my company and employees than I did before. In the big picture, this website is much easier to fix than health insurance. We'll see.

APPENDIX 2: BLOG POST: CREATING A HEALTHCARE.GOV WEBSITE THAT WORKS

Healthcare.gov Suggestions for Improvement

Since I don't like to just complain without offering solutions, on October 14, I wrote a new blog post outlining a solution that would be better for consumers, easier to develop, quicker to test, more scalable, and more secure. Entitled *Creating a Healthcare.gov Web Site that Works (http://blog.fmsinc.com/creating-a-healthcare-gov-web-site-that-works/)*, it offers suggestions:

Understanding the Buying Process for Health Insurance

It's important to understand what the website should do. The primary mistake the designers of the system made was assuming that people would visit the website, step through the process, see their subsidy, review the options, and select "buy" a policy. That is NOT how the buying process works. It's not the way people use Amazon.com, a bank mortgage site, or other insurance pricing sites for life, auto, or homeowner policies. People want to know their options and prices before making a purchase decision, often want to discuss it with others, and take days to be comfortable making a decision. Especially when the deadline is months away. What's the rush?

The existing process acts as if a retail website asked for your credit card number before showing what you could buy and their prices. Almost all sites let you browse without creating a user name. Retailers want you to see what's available as quickly and easily as possible. People often visit multiple times before buying. Only after making a purchase decision should personal information be collected to complete the transaction.

The website needs to reflect this and support a more common buying process.

Conceptual Overview

Here's an overview showing three distinct processes that flow into each other (or people buy a policy at their step and leave the system). A critical part is offering a comparison matrix at each level so consumers can quickly see the differences between the insurance policies.

- Quickly Enter Basic, Non-Personal Info
- See Policies and Prices in a List and Matrix
- Buy or Request Subsidy Estimate

Request Non-Subsidized Quote

- Enter Non-Personal Info
- See Policies and Prices with and without Subsidies in a List and Matrix
- Buy or Apply for Subsidy

Estimate Subsidy

- Enter Personal Information
- Generate Official Subsidy
- See Policy Comparison Matrix
- Buy a Policy with Your Subsidy

Apply for Subsidy

1. The first one gives policy options and non-subsidized quotes. People can click to purchase the policy from the insurance company. If so, they leave *Healthcare.gov* and the Government is no longer involved.

2. The second provides a subsidy estimate and uses the same display as the first but with and without subsidized prices. People can also click to buy the policy without a subsidy and leave the system, or they can officially apply for a subsidy.

3. The third is the actual application for the subsidy and the only path which collects Personally Identifiable Information (PII). Higher security is necessary for this.

The first two do not require PII and would not require high security. That means a commercial cloud service such as Microsoft Azure could be used to host the site and adjust to high traffic loads. It would support people shopping and browsing multiple times before buying without the need to invest in hardware or bandwidth.

With this improved design, only a small portion of the site's traffic would be in the final subsidy application portion. That can be isolated with high security and for much lower volumes of users since people would only apply once. Hassling people at this stage with lots of personal questions is acceptable since people are serious about purchasing.

User Experience Goals

These are some objectives for creating a great user experience:
- Quickly get the unsubsidized insurance rate quotes and policies (no login required);
- Easily compare among insurance policies based on features and price;
- Easily select and subscribe with an insurance company without a subsidy;
- Quickly receive an estimate of a subsidy without having to provide personally identifiable, confidential information;
- Easily compare among insurance policies based on features and subsidized prices;

- Formally apply for the subsidy (log-in and personal information required);
- Select a subsidized policy and pass the appropriate information so the insurance company can validate the subscriber's information and receive the subsidy;
- Once policy options are offered, allow users to create a log-in to save their inputs, and get back into the system to recover their work-in-progress. This would be required with the formal subsidy application but not necessary for the other options.

Technical "Back Office" Goals

- *Performance.*—The system should move people through the process as quickly as possible.
- *Collecting Information.*—It should not ask for any information that's not required for generating the policy options and prices.
- *Fewer Screens.*—Rather than having one screen per question, multiple questions should be asked in as few screens as possible. People know how to scroll. Extra screens should only be added if they depend on answers from previous screens.
- *Data Security.*—The first part of data security is to NOT collect sensitive information. Sensitive information should only be collected from people actually applying for the subsidy.
- *Data Integrity.*—All database changes need to be in transactions with commitments and rollback on failure. Situations where accounts are partially created with a valid user name and no account details should never occur.
- *No Other Connections During Data Entry.*—The system should not be connecting to other data sources while the user is entering data. Just collect the data.
- *Off-line Processing.*—Once the user enters all their data for a subsidy quote, a separate system processes the applications and interfaces with the other systems to validate the data and calculate the subsidy. By separating this process from the user's on-line experience, problems with connections to other systems do not impact the user.
- *Email Notification.*—Once a subsidy is calculated, an email is sent to the user inviting them to log into the system to see their options.
- *Notification to Insurers.*—Web pages and web services to allow real-time views of the status of applications selecting the insurer's policies.
- *Commercial Cloud Hosting.*—Using a commercial cloud platform would provide automatic scalability to meet fluctuating levels of users without having to make hardware purchases. By eliminating the need to collect and store sensitive user data for most of the website, commercial cloud hosting and its benefits are available without security concerns.

Oversight Goals

Management and interested parties should have system dashboards:
- *Real-time Displays.*—Monitor user progress with summary tables and graphs showing the status of people moving through different stages of the system.
- *Basic Business Intelligence.*—Summary and drill-down details by State, date, hour, etc.
- *System Transparency.*—Provide a public view of some data in a cached mode (updated daily or hourly, but not real-time).

Design Overview

Here is how the goals could be implemented for the *Healthcare.gov* website:

(1) The initial form asks people to select their State. If the visitor is in a State that has their own system, ship them to those sites, otherwise proceed with the next step in the Federal system.

(2) Collect the information necessary to create the unsubsidized options. I was told there were five or so pieces of information necessary to generate the unsubsidized rates (e.g. gender, year of birth, family status, smoking status, etc.).

(3) Display the available plans with options to compare and filter them easily based on plan level (gold, silver, bronze, etc.), provider, price, etc. Should be similar to retail websites like Best Buy or Staples showing different products and their features in a matrix comparison, with buttons to get more details and a button to select one to buy. One would expect users to come to this site multiple times over multiple days to learn about their options before making a purchase.

(4) An option to save the inputs. This would be the first time to create a simple account to collect user information (which does not include things like social security numbers, birthdates, or names). A simple user name (e-mail address) and

password, with a standard e-mail confirmation that doesn't have a time limit. This would allow users to get back to the previous screen without re-entering their data.

(5) An option to get a subsidized price estimate. If the person chooses this option, they create a simple account because highly sensitive information will not be collected. The account is simply to retrieve the user's entries. The user provides the information necessary to calculate the prices without having to look up data from Government sources. The user can enter their values for income and whatever other factors impact generating a subsidy estimate. Just like bank websites let you enter basic information to get a mortgage or car loan rate before you apply, *Healthcare.gov* should do the same. This would allow the site to create quotes quickly without having to bog down or wait for the other sites such as the IRS, Experian, etc. This minimizes the impact of too many users. Once the estimated subsidies are calculated, a display similar to No. 3 above would show the options.

(6) Finally, applying for the subsidy. Once someone decides they want a particular policy, they can officially apply for a subsidy. This is the first time personal data needs to be entered. The system should collect the data as quickly as possible without having to validate the information while the user is entering it. Once all the data is collected, the user is informed via email when the subsidy calculation is ready.

(7) A separate background process calculates the subsidy requests and looks up the necessary data from the different sources. If any of those linked systems is unavailable, it's no big deal since it doesn't impact the user on the website. The user is already gone and waiting for an e-mail. Once the calculation is generated (or if it couldn't be generated), the user is notified via e-mail and they can view the results by logging back into their account.

For management, there should be dashboards with tables and graphs showing what's happening. No more excuses of not knowing how many people are in each phase of the process, how many have received quotes or enrolled, etc. For transparency, some of this information should be publicly available updated at least daily.

CONCLUSIONS

I'm not sure whether the people designing and developing the site will find these suggestions helpful. There's obviously lots of details not included in my proposal, but I'm confident my basic design is a significant improvement over the original site. It would provide a better user experience, be much easier and faster to develop, easier to test, and more scalable and secure. Was it that tough to envision earlier?

Let's remember, this website remains the automation of a paper form. It's not as hard as providing health care.

Chairman MCCAUL. Thank you, Mr. Chung. I appreciate your testimony.

Mr. Krush is now recognized for 5 minutes.

STATEMENT OF WAYLON W. KRUSH, CHIEF EXECUTIVE OFFICER, LUNARLINE, INC.

Mr. KRUSH. Chairman McCaul, Ranking Member Thompson, and the Members of the committee, thank you for this opportunity to testify today on the important topic of cybersecurity as it relates to *HealthCare.gov*. I am Waylon Krush, founder and CEO of Lunarline, Inc. We are a leading provider of cybersecurity products, services, and training for the Federal Government and also the commercial sector. I am also a founding member of the Warrior to Cyber Warrior program.

The Warrior to Cyber Warrior program provides, at no cost, a 6-month boot camp for returning veterans. This program equips veterans or their—if a veteran is unable to participate because of service-related injuries, their spouses—with the skills, training, and certifications they need to thrive in the cybersecurity world. I have

been asked to speak today on the topic of cybersecurity as it relates
to the recent events surrounding the *HealthCare.gov* website and
related systems.

I want to make clear that I am not here to weigh on the political
debate surrounding the Patient Protection and Affordable Act. This
is above my pay grade. Instead, I am here in my capacity as a cybersecurity professional, one who has contributed to the defense of
our Nation's IT infrastructure, both as a soldier in uniform and as
a leader of one of our country's fastest-growing cybersecurity firms.
I was recently asked by the press if I would, as a cybersecurity professional, trust my own personal data to *HealthCare.gov*.

I said yes that I would, and I stand by that statement. This is
not because I believe *HealthCare.gov* is 100 percent secure. There
is no IT system, Federal or otherwise, that can make this claim.
Instead, my confidence in *HealthCare.gov* is based on my hands-on
experience with the rigorous process the Federal Government has
instituted to effectively manage—not eliminate, but manage—cybersecurity risk.

Now, I realize it is a bit odd for a cybersecurity professional to
come before Congress and preach the confidence in our Government's cybersecurity posture. We cybersecurity folks are usually
better known for peddling cyber doom and gloom. However, the
truth is there is plenty of cause for confidence, particularly when
we—it comes to Federal cybersecurity. To explain why I feel this
way, I would like to focus my testimony today on the risk management framework and how it relates to some of the concerns recently brought up in the on-going media coverage of
HealthCare.gov.

Now, I have been given just 5 minutes to briefly describe this extensive cybersecurity process and regulations that provide the foundation for the U.S. Government's systems security. To put this task
into context, a few years ago a colleague and I wrote a book entitled, "The Definitive Guide to the C&A Transformation." In this
book, we did our best to scope down thousands upon thousands of
pages of Federal cybersecurity and privacy regulations into 600
pages of easy reading.

The easy reading part is a joke, but the level of depth and rigor
in this process is not. Here today, I will try to distill these processes even further into just 5 minutes of testimony. During these
5 minutes, I will do my best to describe how the 6-step risk management framework supports the Federal Information Security
Management Act. Excuse me.

This, in turn, should provide a baseline understanding for the security processes governing *HealthCare.gov* and, in reality, any Government IT system. I hope that from my testimony this will help
folks interpret how now-famous decision memo originally intended
for Marilyn Tavenner that describes some of the known security
risks faced by *HealthCare.gov*. The RMF is a 6-step process. It includes categorization, security control selection, implementation,
assessment, authorization, and continuous monitoring.

I will briefly describe each one of these steps, and provide some
insight into how each one relates to the security of *HealthCare.gov*.
I will, however, caution the committee that any internal
vulnerabilities related to *HealthCare.gov* should absolutely not be

publicly released until HHS or CMS has time to mitigate or remediate these issues. The first step is categorization. We look at all of the data types that are actually in the Federal information system.

We have two publications, NIST Special Publication 860, Volume 1 and Volume 2. So we have to find out what type of data this system consists of. The next step governs the selection of the security controls. This is a process where we automatically assign a set of baseline security controls, whether it is low, moderate, or high. And enhancements, if need be, based on the protection requirements of the system. In step 3, this is where we actually implement the security controls.

These are hundreds upon hundreds of controls, including enhancements and tailoring guidance that goes into every Federal information system. In step 4, we actually have assessment. These are on-going assessments, these are assessments before the authorization decision is made. These are annual assessments. These are what we call assessments that go with the updates of code that we are gonna see during this process of updating *HealthCare.gov*. There is one thing that we need to know; there is no such thing as a clean assessment.

An assessment of any system, Federal or otherwise, will always reveal some security risk. It is not possible to have a completely secure system. In conclusion, I hate to tell everyone but at this point in time there is no cybersecurity bullet, silver bullet. If there were I would be selling them, lots of them. A secure system requires the right people, process, and technology to work together harder, smarter, and faster than the adversary.

[The prepared statement of Mr. Krush follows:]

PREPARED STATEMENT OF WAYLON W. KRUSH

NOVEMBER 13, 2013

Chairman McCaul, Ranking Member Thompson, and Members of the committee: Thank you for this opportunity to testify today on the important topic of cybersecurity as it relates to *Healthcare.gov*. I am Waylon Krush, founder and CEO of Lunarline, a leading provider of cybersecurity products, services, and training to both Federal and commercial clients.

I am also a founding member of the Warrior to Cyber Warrior program. Warrior to Cyber Warrior provides, at no-cost, a 6-month cybersecurity boot camp for returning Veterans. This program equips Veterans, or if a Veteran is unable to participate because of service-related injuries, their spouses, with the skills, training, and certifications they need to thrive in the cybersecurity world.

I have been asked to speak today on the topic of cybersecurity as it relates to the recent events surrounding the *Healthcare.gov* website and related systems. I want to make clear that I am not here to weigh in on the political debate surrounding the Patient Protection and Affordable Care Act. That is above my pay grade. Instead, I am here in my capacity as a cybersecurity professional, one who has contributed to the defense of our Nation's IT infrastructure, both as a soldier in uniform and as a leader of one of our country's fastest-growing cybersecurity companies.

I was recently asked by the press if I would, as a cybersecurity professional, trust my own personal data to *Healthcare.gov*. I said yes, that I would. I stand by that statement.

This is not because I believe that *Healthcare.gov* is 100% secure. There is no IT system, Federal or otherwise, that can make this claim. Instead my confidence in *Healthcare.gov* is based on my hands-on experience with the rigorous processes the Federal Government has instituted to effectively manage—not eliminate, but manage—cybersecurity risk.

Now I realize it is a bit odd for a cybersecurity professional to come before Congress and preach confidence in our Government's security posture. We cybersecurity folks are usually better known for pedaling cyber doom and gloom. However, the truth is, there is plenty of cause for confidence, particularly when it comes to Federal cybersecurity.

To explain why I feel this way, I would like to focus my testimony today on the Risk Management Framework and how it relates to some of the concerns recently brought up in the on-going media coverage of *Healthcare.gov*.

Now, I have been given just 5 minutes to very briefly describe the extensive cybersecurity processes and regulations that provide the foundation for U.S. Government system security. To put this task in context, a few years ago a colleague and I wrote a book entitled *The Definitive Guide to the C&A Transformation*. In this book we did our best to scope down thousands upon thousands of pages of Federal cybersecurity and privacy regulations into just 600 pages of easy reading.

The easy reading part is a joke, but the level of depth and rigor in the process is not. Here today, I will try to distill these processes even further, into just 5 minutes of testimony. During these 5 minutes I will do my best to inform everyone on how the 6-step Federal Risk Management Framework (RMF) supports the Federal Information Security Management Act (FISMA).

This, in turn, should provide a baseline for understanding the security processes governing *Healthcare.gov*, and in reality any Government IT system. I also hope that my testimony will help folks interpret the now-famous "decision memo"—originally intended for Marilyn Tavenner—that describes some of the known security risks faced by *Healthcare.gov*.

The RMF is a 6-step process that governs the categorization, security control selection, control implementation, control assessment, authorization, and continuous monitoring of all Federal IT systems. I will briefly describe each step and provide some insight into how each one relates to the security of *Healthcare.gov*. I will however caution the committee that any internal vulnerabilities related to *Healthcare.gov* should absolutely not be publicly released until HHS or CMS has time to mitigate or remediate these issues.

The first step, Step 1, is called categorization. During system categorization we analyze all the information stored, processed, or transmitted by any component of the system. We classify all data by data type and sensitivity, and set the protection level as "Low," "Moderate," or "High" to meet the requirements of the most sensitive system data. Based on what I have read publicly thus far, *Healthcare.gov* is most likely categorized as a Moderate system.

The second step, Step 2, governs the selection of security controls to meet the protection requirements defined in Step 1. As a "Moderate" level system, *Healthcare.gov* is required to implement, at minimum, several hundred security controls. Additional controls may be selected based on any unique system security requirements, such as the presence of personally identifiable information (PII).

In Step 3, we take the controls identified in Step 2 and implement them. This is where the rubber hits the road. HHS and CMS have both authored comprehensive information security policies that govern their approach to cybersecurity. These policies are backed by significant investments in enterprise detection and protection capabilities, including security operations centers, enterprise end-point technologies, border and gateway filtering, incident response teams, and enterprise continuous monitoring capabilities. For *Healthcare.gov*, these enterprise-level controls are combined with system specific ones to support the implementation and maintenance of an effective security posture.

After selecting and implementing controls, Step 4 of the RMF mandates frequent security control assessments. These are tests that are conducted to determine whether or not to allow a system to continue operation. However, let me be clear: There is no such thing as a clean assessment. An assessment, of any system, Federal or otherwise, will always reveal some security risks. It is not possible to have a completely secure system.

At this point, everyone here is probably familiar with the "Tavenner memo" I discussed previously. This memo described some components of the "Federally Facilitated Marketplace" that had not yet undergone thorough re-testing due to continued system development. It was determined that this uncertainty represented a "high risk."

Now, there is no denying that this does indeed represent a significant system risk. Had the memo ended with that finding we would have every right to be deeply concerned. However, the memo continues to outline a comprehensive mitigation strategy designed to mitigate this risk. This includes the establishment of a dedicated security team to monitor the system, weekly testing of all border and web-facing assets, daily/weekly scans using continuous monitoring tools, and a promise to conduct a full Security Control Assessment within 90 days.

While *Healthcare.gov*'s political sensitivity has cast a spotlight on this process, these types of risk analyses are common place across the Federal Government. Again, security assessments always reveal risks, no matter what system is being assessed. How those risks are managed ultimately determine whether or not a system can be labeled "secure." There is a reason it's called the "Risk Management Framework," rather than the "No Risk Framework." It is designed to ensure that Risk Executives conduct precisely these types of trade-off analyses.

The Tavenner memo is also an example of Step 5, called System Authorization. Simply put, this step requires a management decision on how, when, and under what conditions a Federal system may be authorized to operate. Like *Healthcare.gov*, most Federal systems are authorized with conditions and pending the implementation of an effective mitigation strategy. This is exactly what you are reading in the Tavenner memo.

Finally, during Step 6 we continuously monitor security posture throughout the entire system life cycle. This is the most important step in the process. This is why I have publicly stated that I would trust my own personal data to *Healthcare.gov*. I know as well as anyone that as soon as a system is developed you are in a race against time to find and mitigate vulnerabilities. This is particularly true for high-value targets such as Government IT assets.

That being said, if HHS follows through with their on-going daily and weekly scanning and more importantly—quickly remediates and mitigates security issues as they are discovered, we can be assured our data is safe as possible.

In conclusion, I hate to tell everyone this, but at this point and time there is no cybersecurity silver bullet. If there were, I would be selling them—lots of them. A secure system requires the right people, process, and technology to work together, harder, smarter, and faster than the adversary.

Chairman MCCAUL. I thank Mr. Krush for your testimony. Yes, I have emphasized before this is probably one of the most significant websites ever created by the Federal Government. In this exchange, the most personal, private data is put into this—Social Security numbers, addresses, e-mails, personal-private health information. I can't think of anything more private than health information. What the American people want, I think, is not only a system that works and that is functional—which, clearly, this is not. As Mr. Chung said, it was amateurish.

But they also want some assurance that it is secure. They do not want this data breached and obtained by hackers, or identify theft perpetrators who can then exploit that information. To that point, the CMS administrator wrote a letter to our committee and, specifically, to the Ranking Member, Mr. Thompson, because of his concerns about security of this website. The assurance was given at that time, when that letter was written, that it would be both secure and follow industry best practices.

We have since found out that a September 3 memo came out from a senior official at CMS stating that it found two high-risk issues and said the threat and risk potential is limitless. According to Federal guidelines, high-risk means vulnerability could be expected to have a severe or catastrophic adverse effect on organizational operations, assets or, most importantly, individuals; individuals being the American people. We have advocated for a delay in the implementation of this law for many reasons.

But certainly, when you have a dysfunctional website and a security risk to the American people's most personally identifiable information, I think that delay, that argument, is certainly even stronger. Mr. Chung, do you agree that we should delay implementation?

Mr. CHUNG. Delaying that would be a policy question. With regard to my knowledge, it would be on the technical side. My expectation would be that when we pay this kind of money to these contractors they would build something that would be secure. It is like buying a car that has tires on it. You would assume that for hundreds of millions of dollars it would be a secure site.

The other part of this would—you know, the first step in security and privacy is to not ask for information that needs to be secured. So going through the process of asking all those personal pieces of information, when people are just shopping, without even buying or requesting a subsidy, is an outrage. I don't know if the identity verification company is getting paid for every person that they verify, but I think if you follow the money it would be very easy to see how those decisions were made.

Chairman McCAUL. In your opinion here, did CMS actually follow industry best practices in setting up this website?

Mr. CHUNG. I was not involved directly on the project so I am not exactly sure what they did or didn't do. I just know from a taxpayer's perspective we paid enough money to demand, and expect, a fully functional website. It is huge how much we have paid. It is over, what, $300 million? I think you can get a 747 and crash it into the ground for less. So it is unbelievable what we have spent for essentially the automation of a paper form.

Chairman McCAUL. So I guess the question is, I mean: How did this come to be? I mean, we spent, you know, all this money for what you called an amateur website. How did that happen?

Mr. CHUNG. I think that we have an environment where Government contractors are incentivized, especially when they know a customer has an open pocketbook, to create opportunities to bill more hours, to put in more features, to add more complexity, get more change orders, and get the next contract. That is the product that they are really going after. It is not necessarily creating a solution that works. They got caught this time because the general public actually use software that they created. But there are a lot of projects in the Government where Government contractors deliver things that the public never sees.

Chairman McCAUL. So in other words, you have a Government-run program that the contractors exploited for their own profit at the expense of the American taxpayer.

Mr. CHUNG. Absolutely. I think that is very clear.

Chairman McCAUL. I am personally stunned that DHS, that has primary responsibility over the dot.gov space—Federal-civilian networks within the Government—the extent of communication with the Secretary and with HHS was two e-mails and one phone call. When I asked a question about how does HHS rank in its scorecard, if you will, for cybersecurity they get a 50 percent compliance record and they rank No. 2 at the bottom.

They are the second-worst Federal agency when it comes to security of their networks. Mr. Krush, don't you believe that the Department of Homeland Security should play a greater role in trying to secure this website?

Mr. KRUSH. I believe they should play a greater role. I will say, however, the process that was followed is the process that is followed with all Government systems. Meaning that a risk-based decision was made by an executive that was put in charge of the site. They were provided the information about what type of vulnerabilities, what things need to be mitigated. You know, this goes on throughout the entire Government.

You know, there is not a system out there that is perfect in nature, by any means, from a cybersecurity perspective.

Chairman MCCAUL. No, this was certainly not perfect. Mr. Chung, if you have a business and you are pushing a product, and your website not only is dysfunctional but it crashes, would you take a time out and try to fix it first? Or would you still go forward with that program?

Mr. CHUNG. I guess it depends how desperate I was. But, you know, being concerned about the experiences of my customers, no, I would not be able to deliver a product that didn't work. That was what was so shocking when I experienced it on the first day. Because I wasn't there to do a quality assessment of that *HealthCare.gov* website. I went there to get a price. It was by accident that I find myself in this situation, after experiencing what can truly be considered one of the worst pieces of software I have ever used.

Chairman MCCAUL. In addition to a bad piece of software, though, you have the security risk to Americans' most private information.

Mr. CHUNG. Absolutely. When you have an environment where the developers can barely get the website functional, security is way down on the list of things to take care of, right? Security needs to be built in at the very beginning, not added at the end. When you have an inexperienced developer—people don't—that can't even build a website properly or spell or do grammar, I mean, the skill set that is necessary to create a secure website are far higher than what I could see was the skills of the people that were put on creating that website.

Chairman MCCAUL. So I guess it comes as no surprise that under 50,000 Americans have actually signed up for the exchanges, given the fact that, No. 1, the website is flawed. No. 2, the security risks are so great, if people—if the administration was really interested in getting more people to sign up you think they would take a time-out, fix this, and also fix it from the security standpoint.

The thing that also bothers me tremendously is that it has been reported to me that there are about—there are over 700 fake websites out there that purport to be an exchange, purport to be part of this Obamacare program. *HealthCare.gov* is the official, but there are over 700 fake websites out there that are preying on victims for their personal identifying information so they can exploit that. Does that trouble either one of you? Mr. Krush.

Mr. CHUNG. That happens all the time on every website. That is not unusual.

Mr. KRUSH. Yes, that is not abnormal. One of the things that were brought up earlier by DHS was that they ensured that HHS actually implemented DNS security. So that if you go to *HealthCare.gov* you are arriving at *HealthCare.gov*. That doesn't take away the process that when you go out to go to Google.com and you actually put a "P" in front of it, or a "G" or something, you are gonna sent to a site that looks like Google but I wouldn't be using that search engine.

Chairman McCAUL. Well, I think it demonstrates—I mean, perhaps a better public education process to demonstrate that there are fake websites out there, and here is the official one. Again, I will close by saying I am troubled that the Department of Homeland Security, that has the primary responsibility for securing the dot.gov space, is defaulting to an agency, a department, HHS, which has one of the worst scorecards when it comes to cybersecurity.

With that, it is lunchtime. A lot of the Members have left. But I do want to give the witnesses, since you have taken so much time to prepare and come here today, perhaps give you the last word. I will start with Mr. Chung.

Mr. CHUNG. Well, thank you very much. I mean, I can tell you that as a small business owner I am facing the need to buy insurance for myself and my employees. I have to follow the law. I don't get to choose the laws that I follow. I was really hoping that this would be an opportunity for me to be able to buy health insurance that would be more competitive. Health insurance is a big problem for small businesses. We pay the highest premiums for the worst coverage.

We are competing against companies like CGI and these other Government contractors that are much bigger and can probably get lower-priced insurance than we can. So I hope that throughout this whole process we do keep in mind that getting health insurance for companies is important to small businesses for us to remain competitive.

Chairman McCAUL. Thank you.

Mr. Krush.

Mr. KRUSH. I would just like to say that, you know, the processes that we have in place in the Federal Government are some of the most rigorous processes of any type of auditing you would perform on any type of information system. I am very familiar with the type of commercial auditing that goes on. I am very familiar with the Federal auditing that goes on. So, you know, the depth and rigor in the implementation of cybersecurity and privacy requirements that we do build into the systems—whether, you know, they are always working properly, or not—is some of the best out there.

I mean, there is just really no comparison. All of the previous speakers brought up HIPAA, they brought up different compliance requirements that are out there. I will tell you, if you are gonna deploy a Federal information system you must not only implement those controls, but the control catalogue itself that we are required to implement throughout each one of the components; whether that be starting at the hardware layer, the hypervisor, the operating system, and all the applications to sit on top of that is the most rigorous cybersecurity of any Nation in the world. Also, just of any organization, whether it be Government or not.

Chairman McCAUL. Well, with all due respect, I would submit, in this case, it was an abysmal failure. We don't like to see that as Americans, and hope we can move forward in a more productive way.

With that, I want to thank the witnesses for your testimony. Members are advised if they have additional questions they can submit that within 10 days. I would ask you to respond in writing to that. Without objection, the committee stands adjourned.

[Whereupon, at 12:45 p.m., the committee was adjourned.]

○

www.ingramcontent.com/pod-product-compliance
Lightning Source LLC
Chambersburg PA
CBHW081846280526
45789CB00007B/2576